Roses under the Miombo Trees

Roses under the Miombo Trees

An English Girl in Rhodesia

Amanda Parkyn

Illustrations by Jayne Watson

Matador
9 Priory Business Park,
Wistow Road, Kibworth Beauchamp,
Leicestershire. LE8 0RX
Tel: (+44) 116 279 2299
Fax: (+44) 116 279 2277
Email: books@troubador.co.uk
Web: www.troubador.co.uk/matador

ISBN 978 1780882 376

British Library Cataloguing in Publication Data.
A catalogue record for this book is available from the British Library.

Typeset in 12pt Adobe Garamond Pro by Troubador Publishing Ltd, Leicester, UK
Printed and bound in the UK by TJ International, Padstow, Cornwall

Matador is an imprint of Troubador Publishing Ltd

For my children and grandchildren

Africa gives you the knowledge that man is a small creature,
among other creatures, in a large landscape

Doris Lessing

CONTENTS

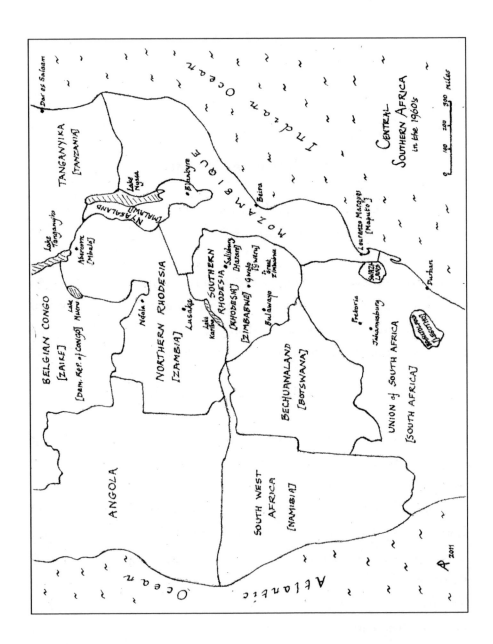

CENTRAL
SOUTHERN AFRICA
in the 1960's

0 100 200 300 miles

BELGIAN CONGO
[DEM. REP. of CONGO]
[ZAIRE]

TANGANYIKA
[TANZANIA]

Dar es Salaam

Lake Tanganyika

Lake Mweru

Abercorn
[Mbala]

NYASALAND
[MALAWI]

Lake Nyasa

Blantyre

NORTHERN RHODESIA
[ZAMBIA]

Ndola

Lusaka

Lake Kariba

SOUTHERN
RHODESIA
[RHODESIA]
[ZIMBABWE]

Salisbury
[Harare]

Gwelo
[Gweru]

Great
Zimbabwe

Bulawayo

MOZAMBIQUE

Beira

Lourenço Marques
[Maputo]

SWAZI
LAND

Indian Ocean

ANGOLA

SOUTH WEST
AFRICA
[NAMIBIA]

BECHUANALAND
[BOTSWANA]

UNION of SOUTH AFRICA
[SOUTH AFRICA]

Pretoria

Johannesburg

BASUTOLAND
[LESOTHO]

Durban

Atlantic Ocean

R. 2011

viii

PREFACE

When my parents moved house for the last time in the 1980's, my mother produced a worn leather document case. 'You'd better have these' she said. It contained the letters I had written home over several earlier decades, hundreds I should think. There were a few in a round, boarding school hand, along with my school reports, then from language college in Switzerland. Most, however, were from various parts of Southern Africa, blue aerogrammes, some decorated with outline sketches of Rhodesian tourist features – 'Visit Lake Kariba', 'Zimbabwe Ruins'. Rustling airmail paper emerged tightly folded from too-small envelopes covered in colourful stamps. I skim-read this collection with a mixture of curiosity and wariness, sorted them firmly into date order, filing them according to period: 'School 1950's', 'S. Rhodesia '59 / '61 – '63', 'N Rhodesia '63 – '65', 'S Africa '65 – '72' and finally 'England '72 onwards'. Then I put them back in their case in the bottom drawer of my bureau.

Some years later I was reading *The Dust Diaries*, Owen Sheers's intriguing memoir cum biography cum travelogue about his ancestor Arthur Shearly Cripps, a maverick missionary and poet in Rhodesia in the early 20th century. It vividly brought back for me the sights, sounds and scents of a country I had known for a few years, but also made me aware of how ignorant I still was about the country's earlier colonial history. I soon recognised that the period in which I had lived there was also significant: for Southern Rhodesia, the die was cast in the 1962 elections for a change of government that would have drastic consequences for the country for years to come. In Northern Rhodesia I had seen the birth of the new Zambia in 1964. Perhaps, I now thought, it would be interesting to see what the letters could say about that period from the point of view of this young English woman.

As I re-read my letters and listened to her voice, the memories I now hold of that period began to intrude, often contradicting or qualifying young Amanda's version written for her parents. I was obliged to confront her racist attitudes born of ignorance and a certain sort of privileged up-bringing. Reading books on the history and politics of the time filled some of the huge gaps in my knowledge of what had actually been going on when I lived there.

I have sought to weave together the voice of young Amanda writing home, the memories I hold now of the time (such as I have been able to access) and my learning about the historical, political and racial context of the era, and thus to offer the reader a journey back to a long vanished era, seen through the prism of a 21st century perspective.

Penkridge, Staffordshire, 2011

The train rocks slightly as it trundles
through the veld. She's looking out on
spindly thorn trees, fawn savannah grass,
the punctuation mark of a fat baobab,
its rootlike branches reaching
to the sky's cloudless, whitish blue.

On the footplate between two carriages
she can smell the dust, hear the engine's
sudden wailing hoot. It slows to walking pace,
stops nowhere - but it's somewhere, people
have gathered, squat on hard beaten dirt,
watch. Swollen-bellied children jostle and point.
The engine hisses steam, pulls slowly away.

In the first class compartment a man in khaki,
knees tanned between drill shorts and thick
long socks, moves to the window, unhitches
its leather strap. He lowers it on warm air,
smell of dust, more veld and thorn trees, more
fawn waving grasses. 'Better get used to that'
he grins, 'M M B A we call it -
miles and miles of bloody Africa.'

PART I
Southern Rhodesia

CHAPTER 1

Bulawayo, where everything was fresh and new

I gazed out over the distant Chimanimani mountains, a glass of Rhodesia's best cold Castle lager in hand, the sun already burning my English winter-white skin. I was 22, just married, the year 1961. My fingers felt for the engraved pattern on my gold wedding ring, the one Mark and I had chosen in Bond Street when he had come over on leave for our February wedding. I wanted to be a good wife, to have a happy marriage, but there was no need to think about how to bring this about, for it would happen, I knew it would.

The barman inside the Mountain Lodge hotel seemed to know what that meant. He would wink at Mark as he opened our bottles of lager, saying encouragingly 'There – a baby in every bottle.' I would giggle and blush and we would take our drinks onto the stoep and plan the next day: a walk in the Vumba hills maybe, or a drive to the border, maybe just more time around the pool. There I would be sure to wet my hair, dry it spread out on a towel on the lawn. I wanted to arrive in Bulawayo as blonde and as tanned as possible. I didn't want people to think that Mark had married some pale little English girl who didn't know the ropes. This was Africa after all, and I badly wanted to fit in.

I knew – or thought I knew – how to do this, for I was not quite a stranger to Southern Africa: in 1959 I had been recovering from a back operation and my mother had thought I needed to 'get away'. (This was to become her default strategy when any of her four children seemed to be at a loose end – send them somewhere). What a splendid idea, she thought, for me to go out to Africa to act as home help to cousin John in Lusaka, whose wife Toni was expecting their second baby. I would have been quite happy to stay in England and persuade the Foreign Office to take me back on to my clerical work in intelligence. The work itself was routine, but London life for a single girl sharing a little flat in SW3 had been enormous fun. But now Mum pressed on, letters were exchanged, and by the time my passage was booked east coast on the M.V. Warwick Castle, I had become quite seduced by the glamour of it: 'I am off to Africa', I would say grandly, with no idea what this would involve, beyond the fun of putting together a hot-weather wardrobe in mid-winter England. After four and a half weeks cruising south, the ship delivered me to Beira, whence I took the train via Salisbury up to Lusaka. In the event, my stay with my cousins had not lasted long, for I did not have the temperament or skills to make a very good nanny/housekeeper to a perfectionist new mother. I loved 15 month old Yvonne, but my pastry would not hold together, and I did not ensure that all the linen was washed every day. After a few weeks embarrassed cousin John said he felt obliged to ask me to leave. He offered to help me find a flat and a job, but Lusaka, though the administrative capital of Northern Rhodesia, consisted of a dusty main street ambitiously called Cairo Road, a few shops, bars and a run down hotel. Visiting politicians and business men stayed at the luxury Ridgeway Hotel well out of town. Whilst I thought about this, would I like a trip to the Victoria Falls, he asked? I would indeed, and had an unforgettable trip on a very slow train across the bush, and marvelled at a multiplicity of rainbows over the thunderous falls. But I returned feeling at a loss, unable to face going home with a sense that I had in some way failed. I had only one other contact in Southern Africa, Mark, cousin of friends at home, who lived in Salisbury. I had met him in England on his university vacations, and on my way from Beira port to Lusaka. Now, hearing my anxious tones on the phone, he leapt to my aid and drove up to fetch me in his old Morris Minor.

How I had loved bright, colourful Salisbury! It may have been derided as 'Surbiton in the bush' as its suburbs with names like Hillside and Borrowdale had grown in the 1950's, but it was far more attractive than that, with its wide avenues lined with jacaranda and flame trees named after British explorers; its modern buildings and parks full of dazzling cannas and hibiscus. Social life for 'company men' like Mark centred around The Club: golf, tennis, drinks after work, impromptu curry suppers. I worked as a clerk for the C.I.D., bought a Vespa for getting around and shared a flat and a sewing machine with a workmate, Margaret Monteith. It was a sort of unintended 'gap year' – though gap between what and what I could not have said. There was still at that time the unspoken expectation for young women that 'career' would mean marriage and family. And so in due course, Mark and I had grown closer. We were opposites: he quiet, I ready to fill any gap in the conversation, his uncritical steadiness an anchor for my anxious temperament. Ours was not a whirlwind romance; our love grew gradually, cautiously even, at a pace I felt safe with. There were times when I had sneaking doubts, wondering 'Is this really right for me?' But the following January we made a slow, scenic drive down to his parents' home in the Cape, Mark's old Morris Minor loaded to the roof rack with us and Cessa, my good friend from London days, over on her own 'Africa tour'. In Cape Town, on the moonlit lawns of Kelvin Grove Club, we had got engaged. The niggling doubts briefly recurred, as I observed how different his family was from mine, wondered how my choice of husband would go down with my parents. But the excitement of being engaged, of choosing the pretty aquamarine ring that the recommended Cape Town jeweller made for me, swept such thoughts away and soon after Mark and I had returned to Salisbury, at my parents' urgings, I reluctantly flew home to wait for the wedding.

Now almost a year later here I was, a married woman, my happiness

5

deepened by a sense that I had done things in my own way. Yes, we had had the wedding my mother thought proper – and very special it had felt too. But here, some 6,000 miles away, I felt free from all the social and family constraints I had been brought up to: the 'right' ways of doing things, keeping company with 'our own sort of people'. No, my parents' language was never as explicit as that, but their meaning was clear to me all the same. Here I can make my own choices, I thought, we can live our life together as we think best.

Right now we were in Rhodesia's Eastern Highlands, close to the border of Portuguese East Africa, a beautiful area later to become notorious for the 'bush war' during the nationalist struggle for independence. It was peaceful, our hotel with its deep thatched roof and leaded windows straight off an English calendar, except for that dazzling swimming pool in a garden full of hibiscus, frangipani and canna lilies and panoramic views over African hills. We made a foray into Portuguese East, as it was known, (now Mozambique) and it instantly felt 'foreign', Portuguese spoken everywhere by both whites and blacks, and a continental meal of which I wrote home later: *at the Café de la Gare we had huge prawns, half a piri-piri chicken and all the trimmings and a whole bottle of white vino for 10/- each – scrum!*

Beside the pool and over drinks, we talked of the future. Mark was a trainee sales representative for an oil company, who must work where he was posted for a junior sales rep's salary and learn on the job. We were about to set up home in Bulawayo, to which he had just been transferred; it was Southern Rhodesia's second city, where I knew no-one. No matter – I felt liberated, launched into my new married life by our big wedding at my parents' home in Surrey, energized by the brightness of the light, the warmth of the sunshine, free of the social constraints and expectations of my English life. We were in love and everything seemed possible.

I too would be learning on the job, and although I would never have thought of it this way, I did bring with me a variety of skills and abilities, some more useful than others here in Southern Rhodesia. Brought up in a comfortable country home, sent to boarding school, then to language

6

and secretarial colleges, I had learned a bit of my mother's rather ad hoc style of cooking – I could make soup from what was in the garden, for example – I could follow a paper pattern and wear the frock I had made, type and organise a filing system. My fluent French and German would surely not be needed, but I knew how to cope while living far from home and make the best of it; and I found it natural to write home regularly, reassuring my parents – and perhaps sometimes myself – that I was fine. Secretly, a large part of me felt pleased to be so far from home, away from my father's critical comments and my mother's unpredictable ways of trying to control me. There had been battles of will with her over the wedding – issues that assumed huge importance, like who should be invited and who should sit where in church. Now I could do things my way, I thought, and Mark, I sensed, would never undermine my fragile self-esteem with hurtful criticisms.

So from a week of peace and quiet togetherness, Mark and I headed back to the real world. Loading up his ageing Morris Minor with luggage that friends had been keeping for him in Salisbury, we set off for our new base, covering the 400 miles in a little under 8 hours along the straight, narrow metalled road. There was nothing much to see on the way, the mountainous scenery of the highlands having given way to flatter bush, punctuated by scrubby trees, hills then no hills, the occasional small town or settlement. Then the cooling towers of Bulawayo came into view, and through its suburbs we came to the home of kind friends of Mark's, Olive and Phil Thompson. Despite their bungalow being crowded with two small boys and with Olive expecting Number 3, they nonetheless found room for us until we had our own place. It was an example of warm, informal Rhodesian hospitality that I found to be wonderfully in contrast with the more formal lifestyle I had grown up in. Phil worked for the railways, an important employer in Bulawayo, and liked to boast that Rhodesia Railways was the only nationalised railway in the world to make a profit. I have no idea if that was true.

Now I wrote to my parents for the first time, thanking them for the wonderful wedding, missing them all but excited about the future – the first of so many letters that Mum kept from that time. It pleased me to be able to write to them about my new life in a strange environment they knew nothing about, to be able to choose what to tell them – and what to leave out, to feel in control of communications between us. My first impressions of this new city were positive:

Byo promises well I think – its quite civilised, I mean not a dorp in the jungle or anything! It hasn't Salisbury's good looks as far as the city centre goes, but the suburbs are quite attractive. Everyone is very friendly, in the shops etc you notice it immediately... I am beginning to feel madly domesticated and home-minded as you may have gathered! ... Being so inaccessible to you is the only cloud in the sky, but I am sure we'll be able to manage to come over not too long hence; we are definitely going to save.

In those early days in Bulawayo, everything felt fresh and new, yet my memories of that time are limited, consisting mainly of a few vivid snapshots, set against some rather vague overall backdrops. The letters I wrote home have filled in some of the missing details of our every day life, such as the names of friends with whom we socialised endlessly. But there are still strange gaps I cannot fill: where did I buy food? was there a local shopping centre? why can't I recall faces, other than those we captured on a few tiny black and white photos? How unpredictable memory is, what tricks it can play!

So building on what I have, here is an early snapshot: I am seeing, for the first time, our 'ain wee hame', (lapsing oddly into Scottish in my first letter home) and I am feeling immense satisfaction that this is *ours*. It stands foursquare, a brick-built whitewashed cottage with a black corrugated iron roof and pillars on a small front stoep (or verandah – a lot of white Rhodesian vocabulary had its roots in Afrikaans, from neighbouring South Africa, whence the early settlers had come). To one side there is a gnarled old tree that looks like one of my father's apples, but cannot be, here in the sub-tropics.

It was tiny, the best our equally tiny budget would allow, given our determination to have a house and a garden, rather than a flat. There were three rooms just big enough for our minimal supply of furniture and a cramped back kitchen with a small electric stove. In my vague memory of it, the garden is limitless – perhaps because it was part of the much larger garden of the main house, whose owners were letting the cottage. Certainly there were shrubs and a few more trees, a large vegetable patch and somewhere at the back, servants' quarters for both the cottage and the big house, a cluster of rondavels (round thatched huts) behind a dense screen of tall bamboos.

My early letters mentioned nothing of this issue of having a servant, but of course we had already decided we would do so, for labour was readily available, and even on our budget, eminently affordable. Africans – black Africans – played a vital part in the lives of white people, but they were so much a part of its fabric that they were for me, so to speak, nothing to write home about. I already knew that they were essential to the running of almost all white households, whose owners did not, therefore, need to worry too much about the absence of mod cons: skimmed and painted cement floors needed polishing, laundry washing by hand, and everything must be ironed on both sides, to kill the putse flies that laid their eggs and which otherwise, I was told, would burrow into your skin. African women were normally only employed as nannies who minded children; 'garden boys' tended flower beds and watered lawns. In town I saw African men employed as delivery boys, drivers, messengers, waiters. Africans were always 'boys' and 'girls', never 'men' or 'women'.

I was not yet quite used to this way of life, writing to my parents early on: *I must stop soon, to walk down to the shops (half mile) to post this, as M has the car ... Most Rhodesian women, note, would send their boy on a bicycle, rather than walk even 400 yards anywhere.*

All my contact with black Africans had, until now, been fleeting: a thank you to someone else's servant or a waiter, encounters with messengers or a garage hand, a brief unsuccessful spell as 'madam' in my cousin's Lusaka home. Now I was to have a servant of my own, cleaning our tiny cottage, working in our kitchen and garden, doing anything we required of him, from bringing us early morning tea to washing up after supper, with a rest period in the afternoons. This was 'normal' to everyone else – but to me felt rather daunting.

Now here was Daniel, small and dark skinned, smiling eagerly and deferentially as we interviewed him on the stoep. He was named, he told me proudly in a soft voice, at his mission school back in Nyasaland, had come south because there was more work here. I am wondering now, how did we find him? Did he come with the cottage, as if left by previous tenants, along with a Baby Belling stove and a frayed wicker chair on the stoep? More likely Mark had put out the word before coming to England for our wedding, and recommendations had been made. The right papers – permits, references – were essential. Mark checked that his were in order, former employers testifying that he was honest and hard working, could cook and clean and work in the garden.

I hoped Daniel would wash regularly, for to me many Africans smelled unwashed, and in my world 'b.o.' was a cardinal sin. There must have been a shower of some sort at the back, in the cluster of servants' 'kayas', but his life there was a mystery to me and I do not recall ever going there, regarding it as somehow foreign territory to me. I was fortunate, for not only did he use the Lifebuoy soap I provided with his rations, but he was skilled at working quietly, somehow managing to keep out of my way well enough in the small space. I watched warily as he padded through the cottage, his broad horny bare feet making no sound on the polished wood floors, his face sweat-shiny as he worked. No need for a polisher, for just like every other servant, Daniel would make them gleam – though not by hand, rather by foot. At first I watched fascinated as he took a large polishing cloth, wiped it into the floor polish tin and folded it into a pad, which he then proceeded to rub over the floor underfoot using a sort of dancing movement. (I secretly tried it myself once, when he was out, but found I could not sustain it for more than a minute and collapsed breathless on the sofa.) In the kitchen I discovered that he was competent at plain cooking – stews, roasts and vegetables – which allowed me to pore over my two cookery books for new and fancier recipes for our supper. Almost all of these involved red meat, without which no self-respecting Rhodesian could get through the day.

Shopping therefore involved not only ingredients for our meals but also Daniel's rations. I can remember being given a leaflet drawn up for new British immigrants, which included advice on employing servants. Doris Lessing quotes from it in her 1957 memoir *Going Home* (she was born and brought up in Southern Rhodesia and returned as a journalist and communist, to report on the situation at the formation of Federation). You were recommended to provide basic foodstuffs weekly:

1½lb of mealie meal a day
½lb of meat a day. This used to be the usual ration, but although the native still looks upon it as his right, the meat position no longer allows it. Other protein foods will then have to be substituted.
Vegetables at least twice a week. This will be found difficult as the African does not understand the meaning of vitamins. He usually likes the more pungent vegetables. Onions, potatoes, cabbage and spinach in limited quantities are recommended.
1lb of sugar per head per week.
1lb of dried peas or beans. These the African does not like. He will always prefer ground nuts, which are usually obtainable. For some months green mealies are available and could be provided.
As much salt as required.
Slice of bread and jam and tea or coffee remaining from the table.

Mark, who had grown up in households with servants, encouraged me to take this advice with a large dose of common sense, for there seemed little point in buying Daniel food he did not want. And despite the leaflet's comments, vitamins or no, he was keen on the vegetables he was allowed to consume from our portion of the back garden, and I'm sure I bought him packets of Tanganda tea and cheap local jam. I remember meat as being very important. The butcher's cuts and prices were whitewashed on his window, largest letters always reserved for the price of 'BOYS MEAT' – in practice rough off-cuts and tough bits such as shin – but meat, mainly lean, just the same. My friend Jiff Bowmaker, who grew up in Salisbury, remembers a sizeable parcel being delivered for her parents' household twice a week. (Jiff's e-mail contrasted sadly with what has been reported from Zimbabwe in recent years: empty shop shelves and near riots when goods were delivered, a boy of 15 and a security guard crushed to death in a stampede to buy sugar in Bulawayo.)

The small size of the cottage struck me again when, like a sudden reminder of the entirely different world I had left, our wedding presents arrived, in two separate consignments. That's another clear memory: a crane preceding a lorry up the drive and depositing a huge crate, weighing 1,000 lbs according to the manifest, in front of our little cottage. The excitement felt like Christmas and birthday rolled into one as I unpacked gifts from mountains of tissue paper and newspaper padding, unfolded the 'trousseau' of linen my mother had insisted on buying me at Marshall and Snelgrove's in Oxford Street, just as, I knew, her mother had for her. Only her mother had not been facing the prospect of saying goodbye to her daughter for an indefinite period. Am I imagining it now, or did I sense her well hidden distress, disguised as extravagance as we chose candy striped sheets, Lan-air-cell blankets, towels (both terry and linen) and ordered monogrammed linen table napkins?

Mark was out, but I at once set to, mit hammer, and by lunch we had all the main bundles out, inc. 4 tea chests. All p.m. was spent sorting, and getting rid of packing material – a vast amount. Final accident tally was: 1 dinner service plate (meat) wh. are obtainable here, no 'weights' to the pressure cooker (15/-) 1 plate missing from the L-J's early morning tea set and worst – 2 claret glasses of Uncle Paul's smashed… but I gather Brierley crystal is obtainable and/or orderable here so I'll try that first. Oh yes, and the sugar-jar from Mrs S's lovely set, and one of Joan W's precious grapefruit glasses … It is amazing how one appreciates all these lovely things now. The lovely linen to sleep on – a bathmat! – a dinner service all smart and nice, and my desk, which I am now at – it has quite changed the sitting room. The kitchen is the difficulty, because it is all the china and glass we shan't be able to fit in when the second 'lot' comes, and the d.room sideboard is full of glass and dinner service! with the [silver] canteen looking v. smart on top.

Mark is going to fix wall shelves in the kitchen to fit a bit more in, but already we have had to pack a few duplicates away. Daniel is fearfully impressed with all our stuff, and seized on the pressure cooker with glee – he knows how to use it which is a relief, as I don't! he keeps saying – Is nice madam, is nice.

With Daniel installed to do everything needed in the house, and with Mark often out of town for the day, I had plenty of time to explore and get to know Bulawayo's city centre. Its particular character is still very clear to me in one of those vivid memories: I am emerging from the shade of one of the arcades of shops that line the downtown avenues, stepping out into the bright burning sunlight and feeling that it is taking for ever to reach the shade on the other side. That long hot walk is due to the decree of Cecil John Rhodes that the original town be built with streets wide enough for the turning of a cart drawn by a full span of oxen. I am not, at this point, very interested in the country's history, though like most recent British immigrants I am aware of the country's close links with South Africa, from whence Cecil John Rhodes's British South Africa Company had driven northwards in its constant search for more mineral rights. Rhodes is still a presence in the city, not only in those spacious streets, but in the form of a large bronze statue of him standing, gazing northwards to lands yet undiscovered. I know that a Land Apportionment Act defined areas of land reserved for whites and for blacks, that blacks were restricted to certain jobs. But if I think about it at all, I reason that this is not South Africa, there's no full blown apartheid here, and our government under Sir Edgar Whitehead is promising reforms that will surely bring greater democracy closer, though not too quickly. Things, I feel, are working pretty well. I do not add, pretty well for us whites.

It was to be some 45 years before I would recognise how little I knew of the country's colonial past, and the extent to which it has coloured the country's politics and development since.

***

From the moment when Rhodes's pioneers raised the Union flag on a hill named Harare in Mashonaland in the name of Queen Victoria, a white administration began the process of making the territory fit for white development. Britain left its management first to the British South Africa Company, authorising it to raise taxes, promulgate laws, set up and maintain an administration and a police force, build roads and railways. So very soon the Masters and Servants Act made it a criminal offence not to obey 'a lawful order of the employer'. When the local people proved reluctant to work for wages – since within their own way of life they had no need for cash – the company found a solution in the Hut Tax, levied on every adult male for himself and each of his wives. To pay it, he would have to work – in the settlers' mines, homesteads or farms. By 1900, both the Shona and the Ndebele people had seen nearly 16 million acres of their traditional lands handed out to the new settlers from the south, leaving them in native reserves on often remote and unfavourable land. Not surprising then, that in 1896/7 both peoples revolted, but inevitably the revolts failed. In the words of Martin Meredith, whose *The Past is Another Country* gives an account of Rhodesia up until the end of white rule:

As the British Government later acknowledged, Rhodesia was established by right of conquest. In their [the revolts'] wake, the whites did indeed bring law and order but not, in the African view, justice, and the memories of the 1896-97 revolt lingered long enough for the nationalists to draw inspiration from it sixty years later.

In 1923, after a referendum of white settlers, Rhodesia became that odd contradiction in terms, a self-governing colony. Britain retained the right to veto legislation that discriminated against the African population, (though it never exercised it until 1965, when Ian Smith's government made its Unilateral Declaration of Independence).

***

By the time we set up home in Bulawayo, the country had been governed for 30 years by a white administration, and had flourished economically,

Balancing rocks featured in John and Toni Watson's Bulawayo garden

welcoming hundreds of thousands of new settlers from Britain after the
Second World War. The city was by now an important railway centre and
had grown into a thriving industrial and business community, albeit with
its nose rather out of joint for being overtaken by Salisbury as the capital
city. Rather to my surprise, I found it had plenty of shops, even two
department stores, Meikles and Haddon & Sly, where I went in search of
replacements for china and glass casualties from our wedding present sets.
There were restaurants, as I wrote home enthusiastically:

*... a gorgeous Italian dinner: I was amazed that one could get such really
good food in a place like Bulawayo – we staggered home groaning of a surfeit
of zabaglione!*
and

... a delicious dinner at a Spanish restaurant, masses of olé and a wonderful paella!

Meikles Hotel with its 'lounge' was important to me: for Mark and his colleagues a few beers after work was de rigeur, but in Southern Rhodesia, as in neighbouring South Africa, women were not admitted into bars where liquor could be seen to be served. So without the hotel's lounge, where drinks could be brought to you by a waiter from a bar well out of sight, these get-togethers would have been off limits for me. City Hall was large enough to host concerts by visiting European orchestras, audiences photographed for the local daily paper, the Chronicle. None of these facilities was available to black residents, who were expected to live their non-work lives in designated areas called 'locations' (with the required permit) or, in the rural areas, 'native reserves' or tribal trust lands. I accepted these arrangements without question because they were there, nor do I recall entering a location more than once – for a display of tribal dancing which I described dismissively as: *... quite amusing but not really spectacular, and of course totally lacking in any organisation or timing!* It wasn't that I was not allowed to enter areas designated for Africans, but that I had no need.

Our weekends were now high points for us both, with tennis and sundowners at the club, braaivleis (barbecues) at friends' homes, the occasional drive into the countryside. Bulawayo beat Salisbury hands down in one respect, for the surrounding landscape is beautiful and more varied than Mashonaland. I was fascinated by the startling outcrops of rock, often weathered into huge spherical shapes and balancing improbably one upon another, which could even be seen in the gardens of some bungalows where they made the ultimate feature.

'We must visit Rhodes's grave,' said Mark one day, and I carefully planned a picnic, visiting a downtown delicatessen for special treats of slices of salami, olives, unusual cheeses and breads to fill our wicker hamper, a wedding gift. We drove the 35 miles or so from the city into the hills known as the Matopos. Here, on a flat outcrop with a panoramic view of African hills lay Rhodes's grave, at the place he called 'The View of the World', where he loved to sit surveying the vast and strange panorama, planning his next moves. He had planned his grave too, specifying the site, the plain granite slab inscribed simply 'Here lie the remains of Cecil John Rhodes'. Close by stood a rectangular stone monument to the men of the Shangani Patrol, killed by King Lobengula's men in 1891. We admired the bas relief panels of figures, some on horseback, some marching, all shouldering rifles, their broad-brimmed felt hats tipped against the sun. History books say that the grave used to be guarded night and day by an African soldier, but I do not recall that when we were there. Nonetheless the site had a solemn, heroic feel to it, a sense of the greatness of empire. I did not know that the Matabele called this hill Malindidzimu – place of spirits – and buried their kings nearby. Nor could anyone have foreseen the atrocities witnessed in the area, when in the early 1980's it was to be at the centre of sustained and savage massacres of the Ndebele people on the orders of Robert Mugabe (himself a Shona, and perceiving them as disloyal). The special force used was his notorious Fifth Brigade, trained by the North Koreans.

On that Saturday, though, this was a place of peace, as Mark and I picnicked among the scattered balancing rocks, under the shade of scrubby musasa trees. Opening the hamper, we undid the leather straps for our plates and cutlery, unwrapped our lunch from tea cloths and cracked open our cans of cold Castle lager. We had the place to ourselves, and as we munched on our tasty treats, I felt a great sense of closeness and security with my new husband. In the warm sun, and with the falling notes of little collar doves in the trees, I was suddenly conscious of being entirely happy, certain that this feeling of companionable contentment would last for ever.

That newly-wed happiness made it all the harder to get used to the demands of Mark's job. Within weeks of our arrival in Bulawayo he was 'on the road', often away for several nights a week, leaving me feeling lonely and bereft. Before he started his travels, we had burglar bars fitted to the bedroom window, although I do not recall ever worrying on that score – it was more the loneliness that I dreaded, and the feeling that the night was alive all around the cottage. It helped that other company wives had to cope on their own too, but still, it was hard:

Today (Monday) Mark has gone away till Thurs. night which is very dismal – Beit Bridge this time, last week it was 2 nights and I spent one night with Brenda H, a rather pale sad looking company wife with a husband quite the opposite, who is away most of every week and she gets lonely and is nervous at night. This I found I wasn't, you'll be glad to hear. The cottage is so compact one's imagination can't run riot! But the days seem rather aimless with no evening with M to look forward to, and not working yet (boring search continues). But I visit various bods like Olive T or Thelma, and even Daniel is company really. I showed him the wedding photos and he was delighted, saying how smart the baas looked, and me looking like Simon [my middle brother], *and the big car, church etc etc – cries of ah and oh!*

I enjoyed his admiration as I relived our great day through the album. I wonder now what Daniel must have made of it all, the black and white photos of men in morning dress and carrying – mostly not wearing – top hats, of women in furs and hats with veils, the beribboned Rolls Royce, the awnings and marquee – all in the grey light of a cloudy English February day.

African Wild Life

She'd been prepared for ants, but not
for these purposeful columns filing daily
towards the garbage bin, penetrating
her kitchen cupboards. They ring the jam pot,
seethe in the sugar bowl.

Nothing knows its place; caterpillars process
nose to tail, their bristly bodies looping
along the polished floor of her stoep.
Cohorts of chongollolas – giant centipedes –
march in black lines across the bathroom,
up the front steps, along a window sill.
And worst of all, at night the baleful frogs
breach the front steps and hop towards the light.

Perhaps, she thinks, as she watches
the houseboy's broom disperse them,
they are outriders for some great army
massing its forces out there, determined
to reclaim its territory.

CHAPTER 2

Of money, and learning to live with loneliness

Money – or our lack of it – dominated those early days, every penny counted. For example, we did not have a phone in the cottage, nor could we afford one, even though Mark was now away overnight quite often. My mother was so horrified to learn that I had to walk down the road to ring him in the evenings, unless I was staying with another lone wife, that she promptly sent us the £11 needed to have one installed. However, we soon discovered that his being 'on the road' actually helped our tight budget … *as apart from having free car and petrol, he gets £60 imprest per month for travelling expenses, which cuts down home expenses while he's away to almost nothing.*

I had started to scan the Bulawayo Chronicle for jobs soon after we arrived, but without a decent shorthand speed I did not come up to scratch for the numerous personal secretary posts available. I was becoming discouraged, longing to fill my days with something more than waiting for Mark to come home when, unexpectedly, I was called for interview at an American firm, Remington Rand, in a downtown outlet for their safes, typewriters and electric shavers: *I was interviewed along with a lot of efficient looking women, so I <u>never</u> expected to get the job – but next day I* *heard that I had! It has the best salary I'd been offered in Byo – £50 p.m. with prospects of a rise. So today I was once more a working girl. The girl I'm replacing is staying a few weeks, so I'm learning from her – typing, telephone, filing, banking, reception – she is <u>incredibly</u> idle – v. Rhodesian-female type... My salary will be a help, for us to be able to save it.*

Although I knew nothing about fireproof safes or electric shavers, the work suited me rather well. My 'hopelessly inefficient' predecessor left me plenty of scope for organising things better, and of the two young bosses, one, Mr Brown, seemed to be permanently off sick, while pale Mr Courtney with his floppy blonde hair was constantly harried by Head Office. In the showroom were fireproof safes, typewriters and sharp, thin-faced Marlene in charge of the shaver counter. Out at the back the African employees – messengers, porters, drivers – congregated in their brown overalls, waiting for orders and laughing and talking over their tea mugs. I learned later, from one of the salesmen, that they had nicknames from the animal world for all the white staff. Marlene, he told me, was 'the chicken' and it suited her perfectly. 'What's mine?' I asked innocently, but the sales rep looked embarrassed and would not tell me. Here, yet again, was a strange, foreign world just out of my reach, incomprehensible. I worked in an office upstairs, where Mr. Courtney came to rely on me. I wrote home happily: *I seem to deal with everything and literally never let up all day, sometimes can't make the cloakroom at all, but do enjoy it...* and for me the bustling city centre gave an impression of living in a vibrant, buoyant economy. However, this was an illusion, for changes were afoot – in fact had been for some years, if only I had paid attention to the country's recent history.

***

As far back as the 1940's the idea of a political and economic federation between the two Rhodesias and smaller Nyasaland (Malawi today) had been explored by the British Government. It saw federation as a way of protecting all three territories from falling under the influence of South Africa's now Nationalist government and establishing a progressive form of 'colony'. Whites described it as 'partnership' – meaning economic progress and rising living standards, guided for the foreseeable future by whites. For black nationalist leaders – who had never been consulted – partnership should have meant equality and a real say in their own destiny. But the British government had pressed ahead and by 1953 there were four governments, four governors, four civil services, one for each country and with the Federal 'layer' based in Salisbury, the whole almost entirely staffed by whites. However, it was only seven years later that Britain's Prime Minister, Harold Macmillan, was speaking to the South African parliament in Cape Town in early 1960, and his words continued to echo around the Federation:

... the most striking of all the impressions I have formed since I left London a month ago is of the strength of this African National consciousness... The wind of change is blowing through this continent and, whether we like it or not, this growth of national consciousness is a political fact.

***

There was much talk of this speech among us whites, the fact that Macmillan had chosen to make it in South Africa, Southern Rhodesia's great ally, somehow giving it added resonance. But I don't recall believing that it applied to us. Surely the government had control of unruly nationalists well in hand, with a raft of new laws, the banning of the African National Congress and detention of hundreds of 'troublemakers'? At the same time, look how petty discrimination had been eased! Blacks could go to the cinema now, enter larger hotels, send their children to private schools, apply for jobs in the civil service. The Prime Minister, Sir Edgar Whitehead, was confident that these measures would appeal to the black middle class, and that they would register to vote in elections planned for the end of the following year, and support his United Federal Party's plans for slow – prudently slow – progress towards full democracy. All of this felt reassuring to me and I brushed aside any niggling indicators of an economic downturn, of falling confidence amongst white people.

As if to reassure me further, a big event during our time in Bulawayo was the Central African Trade Fair. After eight years of federation Southern Rhodesia in particular had flourished economically, benefiting from Northern Rhodesia's mineral wealth, and the trade fair – a coup for Bulawayo over its rival Salisbury – was perhaps an indication of that. I described in my letters how busy the city had become, with *all business firms in a fever, and big noises coming down and chivvying poor harassed Mr C.* Of course we all made much of this event, visiting the fair's stands after work, even tasting wine: *the standard is amazingly high, especially the international stands, except the Iron Curtain ones which are dreary and cheap looking. We've hardly been in in the evenings for supper, usually a hamburger there. Daniel seems to hold the fort alright.*

There was much company entertaining during the fair: Mark and I played host to friends of my parents-in-law, he a retired director of the company, taking them out to the Matopos. On the back of this we got invited to cocktails at the company's fair stand: *I wore my going away suit – a great success. A v. smart do on the lawn, full of v.i.p.'s and ending up dinner for 12 at the Fair's Grill Room. Felt a bit decayed today!*

I feel a pang of regret now that I did not keep that going away suit, made for me in a very light, sapphire blue wool, with a stand-away collar and three quarter sleeves and lined with a patterned blue silk matching the blouse beneath. I like to believe it would have looked good even now, 45 years later.

Life settled into a happy routine, my job keeping me mercifully occupied during Mark's many absences. Daniel kept house far better than I could have done, with floors, furniture and our wedding silver polished to a high shine, the vegetable patch productive. If Mark was away for more than two or three nights, I would stave off loneliness by spending one with one of the other young wives also on her own. At weekends we had started to work on the garden and were slowly creating more basic storage to meet the demands of our enormous stock of wedding presents. My father's old Consular Service tin trunk made a fine linen press at the end of our bed, standing on a wooden base run up by Mark and with my newly sewn patchwork cover. Mark demonstrated how easy it was to make bookshelves out of planks of sapele mahogany and clean bricks. And as we socialised more and more, playing tennis, golf, bridge, swimming, eating with friends, as my tan darkened and my hair bleached in the sun, I began to feel I belonged – that I fitted in, no longer seen as a despised English 'rooinek' [red-neck], those ignorant Brits overseas who 'don't understand the situation over here'. I was becoming adept at picking up the Southern African twang, the 'ja' for yes, the 'ag man' (pronounced 'ach men') with 'men' used on men, women and children alike. I enjoyed using some of the pithy phrases lifted from the Afrikaans, but I did not trouble myself with learning any words in the local language.

Most of our entertaining was relaxed and informal, though for those given to throwing lunch and dinner parties it was easy to do well, with competent servants, spacious stoeps, pleasant, well-tended gardens, perhaps a bar by the swimming pool. Some older established residents could be quite grand: I recall a rather formal lunch party in Salisbury, with servants in whites with scarlet sashes, a perfectly risen cheese soufflé passed round, and for second helpings another one, also impeccably timed. We were not in that league of course, but with our little house full of wedding gift china, glass and silver, I felt honour bound to use them, consulting my two cook books and remembering my parents' example of how to do it. But we – and I am sure our guests – far preferred the casual, out of doors way of doing things, with a reliance on the 'braaivleis' (barbecue), with much inexpensive meat, spicy South African boerewors sausage and salads. I soon learned to whip up a quick anglicised 'spag. bol.' for a few friends after drinks at the company club. The South African drinks industry kept Southern Rhodesia's whites well supplied with affordable wines, brandy and 'sherry', and their brewers had established their Castle and Lion brands of lager in the colony. (Africans, however, were forbidden access to any of these, being restricted by law to 'kaffir beer', a brew derived from maize and sold in the townships in vast beer halls).

I don't remember our discussing whether, or when we were going to start a family. This must sound particularly odd to those who have never known a world without reliable, available birth control. I knew that sex – well, sexual intercourse, not the fun of premarital heavy petting – came after marriage. (My mother had been required to apprise me of the facts of life before I went to boarding school aged 9, and had done it well enough, memorably adding: 'I know this may seem strange to you now, but married people enjoy it'.) The message had stuck and I had been well prepared to 'keep myself for marriage' which, from my upbringing, meant marriage followed pretty quickly by having and raising a family. I never questioned that this was what was expected of me, giggling happily, 'Oh, we'll breed like rabbits!', envisaging myself as Mum at the centre of a large and happy family. So in those early months of our marriage, it was as if I was waiting for pregnancy to happen to me. Yet once my body's changes told me, and the doctor had confirmed that yes, I was expecting a baby, I felt delight but also astonishment – could I really be capable of this? What a pity that the letter to my parents announcing the news of their first grandchild has been lost, along with several others during the first half of my pregnancy. Our becoming parents seemed to me like a natural development in our marriage, bringing with it the job I had been brought up expecting to do. I felt pleased with myself, enjoying the inevitable fuss and congratulations. I was fit and well, suffered little morning sickness, and 'the bump' as we referred to it took a while to show. My only worry was the risk of twins (my father's mother was a twin) and the double demands that would bring. But reflecting on it now, and re-reading my letters with their litany of worries about making ends meet, I think that this turn of events must have been quite scary for Mark who was just setting out on his career. There was, after all, no question of my working once the baby came, so we would be dependent on his small salary.

Meanwhile I happily got on with my job, sorting out the chaotic office systems, looking after harassed Mr. Courtney, saving my salary. It was at work, bent over a filing cabinet, that I first felt deep inside me a tiny unfamiliar flicker of movement. I froze, it came again: this must be the baby, I thought, and then: but it feels like the pat of a kitten's paw. How do I know it <u>is</u> a baby? Perhaps I'm carrying kittens, even puppies? This worried me terribly for a while, though I never told anyone of my fears, my imaginings of a tiny litter. These faded with ensuing check-ups, but the baby's movements remained a huge thrill.

Then Mark was promoted. This brought both good and bad news: more money of course, progress up the career ladder. But he was to cover a new area on his own, based in Gwelo, (now Gweru), a smaller town in the agricultural midlands between Bulawayo and Salisbury. It would mean moving house only two months before the baby was due, and we knew no-one there. Worse, Mark had to take over the area weeks before our move, spending Mondays to Fridays there, our precious weekends truncated. Standing on a platform of Bulawayo's railway station early one Sunday afternoon, waiting for the train that would take Mark away from me, I felt suddenly daunted by the sudden change to our life, and utterly miserable. Back in our empty cottage, Daniel off duty till next morning, I sat down at the oak bureau Granny had given me and wrote home: *He won't be back until Saturday lunch if we're lucky. He had to go so early as he couldn't get a lift, and the later train arrived at midnight. So I saw him off in boiling sun on a totally empty train after an early lunch, and already feel he has been gone months. It was very odd having Sunday by myself, I went to evensong, and then he rang to say he had arrived safely, so that was nice. He only has this week for 'handing over' by Dick H. so I gather they will be away most of the time in the bush, and I don't expect to hear much from him. Dick and Brenda return [to Bulawayo] next weekend, so after that M. will have to find his own way round. He is no more pleased than I am that we shall hardly glimpse each other until the end of October. But it is worth our while for me to stay at work. We hope he may find a house too, so Daniel, the furniture and I can move direct from here. However, in the meantime, the weeks are going to seem very long, though in fact I have got quite a lot to do. Also, the hot weather by now is making me want to rest quite a lot. It has been pretty warmish, and I shall be rather glad to graduate to mornings only next week.*

I was heavily dependent on the idea of Daniel coming to Gwelo with us, though I don't recall asking him if he would. Perhaps for him it would just be another new place far from his Nyasaland home, and he was after all in employment, in a job with reasonable pay and conditions in the context of the time. I felt reassured that, while everything else would be strange and new, I could rely on him to help me set up another home.

We had by now made firm friends with several couples, who were a great support. John and Shirley Macdonald were proudly Scottish and one evening Shirley and I researched, in my Mrs. Beeton, how to make haggis, which she longed for. However, it required one sheep's paunch and pluck (liver, heart and lights) and once we reached … *soak the paunch for several hours in salt water, then turn it inside out and wash thoroughly* our nerves failed us and we gave up on the project.

They and many other couples were kind to me during those weeks, and another way of dealing with the loneliness was by keeping busy, always my instinctive strategy in difficult times. I can see myself now, bent over the old electric Singer, its needle clunking along the seams of a cotton skirt with a large elasticated waist. Edges were pinked – no zigzags on my sewing machine. Finally it had to be 'full regalia' as I described it: full cotton smock tops over skirts with a large U scooped out to accommodate my growing belly, for the great thing was modesty – hide your changing shape, which was somehow indecent. This burst of sewing was one way of meeting the endless challenge of making do on very little: I would buy fabrics from an Indian wholesaler, choose a paper pattern that could be adapted five different ways, and spread it all out on the dining table. Later on baby nighties, cot sheets, curtains, all came off that old machine; nothing was bought if I could make it.

At downtown Remington's offices, I was relieved now to be working mornings only, my future replacement and I *'working like mad things. The office is not in very good spirits just now – like many other firms we are having to economise in a big way, in fact the existence of the branch depends on the profit or loss of the next few months I gather. Consequently Mr. C is harassed, the salesmen are depressed because other firms are undercutting them, the Africans cross because their free tea has been stopped and a new Government tax imposed, and I sad because nothing seems much fun without Mark.*

This was my first mention of an economic downturn which even I could not fail to acknowledge had well and truly set in, triggered by the growing political uncertainty. We all talked about it, endlessly, speculating about outcomes, telling tales of falling house prices in the best suburbs, of people who had flitted away, leaving their building society to do the best they could with an empty property. Looking back at the situation now, one might think Mark and I would have been worried for our future there, but we were not, or at least I wasn't. We had the incurable optimism of youth still on our side, and anyway as far as I was concerned, these attacks were initiated by troublemakers, and we could rely on our government to sort them out, as it had done in the past.

Immersed in my new life as I was, it was strange when, occasionally, an unexpected memory of my faraway 'home' brought it disconcertingly close. One afternoon we were visiting Reg and Jeanette, proud owners of a television, which of course was on. We sank onto the settee for this rare treat, watching a documentary following a pair of champion British ice skaters. Here they were, practising on the Queens ice rink in Bayswater; *Oh look!* I exclaimed, *I skated there in the evenings last winter!* At that moment, among the throng of skaters I appeared, earnestly balancing my way along, coming quite close to the camera. It is the only time I have seen myself on television and it was very strange to do so sitting in that brightly sunlit sitting room thousands of miles away.

The second coincidence was more unsettling: Mark and I were walking under a shopping arcade in downtown Bulawayo, rounded a corner and came face to face with three uniformed British Army officers. I recognised one of them instantly as an old boyfriend of mine, John. Before I had left England back in 1959 for my ill-fated au pair jaunt, we had been mad for each other. But we had fallen out at a dance, with jealous accusations on his part, inarticulate embarrassment on mine, and we had never made it up. All this flashed through my mind in an instant on that hot sunny street, making my stomach lurch. I made a split-second decision to cut him dead and we walked on.

The Illustrated Mrs Beeton, Updated

They decide to give a dinner party – a thank-you
to kind friends. She knows how it should be done:
three courses, the table laid with silver from the canteen,
crystal glasses, candles, the monogrammed napkins.

She leafs through Mrs Beeton (the new edition, 1960).
'*Hors d'oeuvres*' it says, '*present an opportunity
for the cook to show her skill and originality*'.
She remembers her mother's liver paté, served with toast.

'*Plain roast chicken should be accompanied
by thin brown gravy, bread sauce, bacon rolls,
with watercress to garnish, and veal forcemeat stuffing.*'
She'll skip the stuffing, and veg. from the garden will do.

Black and white photos show hands making pastry, sifting,
rubbing, rolling, cutting decorative trims. Colour Plate 39
displays a lemon meringue pie, its peaks lightly gilded.
She settles for swiss roll trifle with canned apricots.

The table settings sparkle. In the steaming kitchen
Daniel in his clean whites clatters pots, as she calls
their cheery guests from the stoep. The paté cuts
neatly. Now she can sip the red her husband's poured.

He sharpens his knife with long strokes, slices of chicken
fall whitely, and now his fork probes for stuffing, pulls forth
a plastic bag of giblets. She joins in the laughter, passes
bread sauce and gravy, flees to the kitchen,

where she snaps at Daniel to hurry with the carrots.
The back door opens on black night full of the shrilling
of cicadas, a chorus of frogs, the smell of warm rain.
Suddenly she's remembering the long pale dusks of home.

CHAPTER 3

Gwelo: 'between one horse town and city proper'

In Gwelo, weary of viewing soulless square bungalows set on small suburban plots, Mark had been networking among his new customers. Now he phoned me with news of something different, sounding excited: 'Come up and see it, he said, it's big, and out of town, you'll love it – but we're going to have to convince the owners we can look after it properly!' On a ridge well out of the town, above a road that led to the airfield and not much else, the car crunched up a long stony drive. Here was another brick built, rectangular, iron roofed house with a long front stoep, this one much larger than our cottage, with spacious rooms on a substantial plot of land, from which no neighbouring homesteads were visible. Its owners, Mr and Mrs Cummings, were an older couple who were off to start a small farm from scratch. They gave us lunch – I remember bountiful salads from their vegetable garden – and it was clear that the place meant a lot to them. We love gardening, we said, admiring the flower borders below the stoep, the big lawn, a vegetable garden and hen run in a clearing in the bush to one side. These last were overlooked by the servants' quarters, the 'kaya' – another, smaller, brick and iron construction. Yes please, we said, trying to look capable, we would like to rent it on a monthly basis – and where can we buy some hens?

We passed muster, to our great delight, and just in time by the end of October the removers came and packed up. Daniel and I stacked trays of seedlings in the car boot, and with a last affectionate look at our little cottage, I turned the old Morris Minor north-east to our new life in the Midlands. We were leaving behind the friends we had just made, Mark was settling into his new sales area, I was seven months pregnant and Daniel's workload – though I don't believe I considered this much at the time – was about to double.

Our homestead, as I think of it now, was the best thing for me about Gwelo, which itself held no attractions. The town fell between two stools in several ways – between Salisbury and Bulawayo, between Shona and Ndebele tribal lands, between one horse town and city proper. Founded in 1894 by Dr Leander Starr Jameson as a staging post between the two larger settlements, it had become – and remains – the centre for the agricultural midlands, with its fine cattle-ranching country, all allocated then to white farmers who, with a scattering of mines, made up Mark's new customers. Railway lines criss-crossing the country converged here, with rail links to Portuguese East Africa (now Mozambique) to the east, South Africa to the south and Bechuanaland (now Botswana) and South West Africa (now Namibia) to the south-west. The two big employers were the Bata shoe factory, which had its own tannery, and a chrome smelting plant. As for the town centre – more relevant to my life – no wide tree-lined avenues here. Its key landmarks were its historic Stock Exchange and the memorial clock tower which Widow Jean Boggie, a great character locally, had had erected in memory of her husband in 1928. The Meikle brothers owned a small department store and the Midland Hotel and there were a couple of other hotels and two restaurants which we subsequently decided were 'decent'. For the rest, the general stores, shaded by corrugated iron arcades, had a frontier town feel to them. Throughout our stay there, I lived for the occasional chance to shop in Bulawayo or – an even greater treat – Salisbury.

Out at our homestead though, all was peace, quiet and long African views over the scrubby bush – though we discovered that the peace could be shattered by low flying Hunter jets from the nearby Thornhill Air Force Base. The house was called 'Norwood', strangely redolent of some English suburb, the area Umsungwe Block, hinting at the original intention of a housing development, now shelved. Behind it ran an already overgrown dirt road still awaiting its share of new bungalows.

I felt like a proper home-maker, and whilst Mark was out on the road in his new area, for me running our new home became an absorbing challenge. We soon realised that we were going to have to get used to the demands of running a much larger establishment. The house, though spacious, had no mod. cons. and was a succession of large bare rooms, in which our small stock of furniture looked somewhat lost. Daniel's day started first, with lighting the wood fired boiler for hot water for Master's shower, then getting our breakfast, so Mark could be off to work by 7.30 or so after his early morning run. Then Daniel would get on with the housework, with acres of red skimmed cement requiring his foot polishing routine. Whilst Daniel worked indoors, I was often out in the garden, settling our seedlings into gaps in the borders, trying to get to grips with the hens, which, like my mother before me, I secretly hated: *It is amazing how busy I am all the time around the place, quite apart from Christmas and babies. The hens have been very tiresome, the other day they began to have an egg-eating orgy; fortunately I was in the veg. garden at the time and noticed what they were up to. Then the mother hen went for me because I was too near to her chicks, so altogether I am fed up with them, and if they didn't lay such nice eggs would cheerfully eat the lot. A battle is also being waged against cutworm, which appear in the night and senselessly destroy the poor little seedlings I have planted out. I am now armed with deadly poisons which I sprinkle liberally, but they are unimpressed. Scrattling about in the garden is my main form of exercise these days – I have been feeling very energetic, mainly I think because of the cool weather. On Sunday Mark even left his work to dig furiously in the veg. garden, and to build compost! It is lovely here at the weekends. We also put up our name sign outside the gate, très eyecatching.*

By now the rains had started in earnest and the garden and surrounding bush sprang into new green life. It relieved me of some of the burdens of watering, certainly, but brought other problems; weeds sprang up overnight, mud trekked relentlessly into the house and the welcome freshness turned to cooler, 'horrible' weather. Perhaps too Daniel's heavier workload had started to take its toll, for I wrote: *Daniel has a cold and cough, but what good giving him medicine when he then paddles in the rain with bare feet? Today it is pitch dark and pouring rain, so I went to get the milk [from a neighbour] in the car, fearing he may get pneumonia. He won't go to bed, we think it makes them think they must be dying.* (I have no idea where we got that idea from or whether there was the least truth in it).

With not much more than a month to go before my expected New Year's Day date of delivery, I was eyeing the baby's bedroom with some anxiety: *Mark has been working so hard and long that he hasn't had a chance to do anything round the house for ages. He seems to come home every night with another report to write. However, we are going to paint the inside and out of the built-in cupboard in the nursery, as it is too scruffy at the moment, and are buying a plain wood table from someone who is leaving Gwelo which I can also paint (for changing etc.) Then I feel the room will be more respectable. Still trying to track down a nice 2nd hand pram if I can.* On our budget I worried about the cost of assembling a basic layette, but fortunately was beginning to receive welcome parcels of baby garments from family and friends in England: tiny hand-knitted cardigans, embroidered nighties. In the heat of the day, when I couldn't be in the garden, out came the Singer and I set about copying what I could. All that was left to do was find dozens of nappies, ideally from a wholesaler.

On top of all that, Christmas was a constant worry and posting dates looming: *Gwelo shows itself daily more horrible for shopping, both for the baby and for Christmas presents, over which I am having a great struggle for that reason. I shall obviously miss the last date for posting, so you had better expect a late gifte anyway! In a fit of energy I managed to get off our cards in time, so that's one thing.*

It is a wonder to me now that with all that we could find the energy for socialising. But of course it was vital to make the most of any promising contacts in order to build some sort of a social life. For us this started with other company couples, though there were far fewer of these than in Bulawayo. Still, on only our second weekend there, a Saturday night braaivleis (barbecue) with Doug and Fran ended at midnight, and next morning Noel and Bridget were calling with a huge basket of apricots. We felt pleased to be able to reciprocate with eggs.

Then we had a windfall: the opportunity for an otherwise unaffordable trip to Bulawayo, with a night at the company's expense, as the General Manager was coming down. There was a social evening followed by a profitable day for us both: *Mark saw Mr. T in the office, and was told that he was doing very well… I had a somewhat energetic a.m. shopping. We found our wholesaler, and with a company order got nappies, plastic bath, oddments and the offer of a very nice pram when we want it (had no room in the car). I also found other odd things like a cot mattress for when Mark makes it and suchlike, all of which far cheaper than here, and your Christmas present… We finally got back here for supper, feeling we had achieved quite a lot. I had left Daniel a list of things to do in our absence, he seemed quite worn out! I am glad to say he is working well now touch wood, having recovered at great expense to me for medicine from his cough and flu.*

By now I was much more aware of my pregnancy, even allowing myself a rest after lunch with a library book. One was of baby names, for Mark and I had no favourites in common, which was a great worry. 'Not Nicholas,' he said firmly, pronouncing it Nicholarse, whilst I barred John as 'boring – anyway he's your brother'. Eventually I suggested we each make a list of our top ten names to see where they overlapped, which resolved the problem – just. My doctor in Bulawayo had handed me over to a friend in Gwelo: *He has pronounced me fit as a flea … I have got to the stage of making long lists of things to do, and hoping for the best! I have supposedly only got 5 weeks to go as from yesterday, so am beginning to feel that I am getting somewhere. No doubt this will soon turn to impatience and 'a feeling of frustration' as the book warns me!!*

The book was Doctor Benjamin Spock's *Baby and Child Care* which was to be my constant adviser. Looking again at the yellowed pages ('the most widely recommended handbook for parents ever published – over 20 million copies sold') I am reminded of how comforting he was: it was ok to have mixed feelings about the baby, to regret losing your sylph-like figure and saying goodbye to your carefree youth … love for the baby might come only gradually … you were bound to get tired, even blue, and would need some help in the first months … fathers might well feel left out, but a man could be a warm father and a real man at the same time … grandparents might, or might not be a source of support and help in the early weeks. It was all very reassuring in its way. But for live support I had to rely on a few very recently made woman friends, almost all of whom, helpfully, had babies and/or toddlers. There were no ante-natal classes available, but someone lent me a booklet on natural childbirth, with instructions for breathing and relaxation, which I practised dutifully (but which turned out to be of precious little help when it came to it). The Birchenough Nursing Home ('very small, only holds 14 at most, nice and quiet') had given me a list of needs to pack for what would normally be a ten day stay, prompting me to run up, 'out of my head', a quantity of nighties on my hard working Singer.

My poor parents must have been worried silly when I wrote in some detail about my car accident:

I escaped with no harm to me but quite a lot to the car. I was shopping in town, and a landrover backed out of a parking place at the side of the road into me. Fortunately I was travelling at about 2 mph, but the whole of the left front wing is ruined (landrovers being so solid). A policeman was on the spot and said it was my fault, which I couldn't believe, and sure enough a superior finally came and said of course not, and the other chap was fined for negligent driving, so he is going to pay the £23 damages. Mark had just left for the day to go into the bush and isn't back yet, so I rang Doug C from the office of the Gwelo Times who had sat me down and given me water etc., and he managed everything very nobly. All well now.

The policeman on the spot would have been an African constable, his superior a white officer, their force the British South Africa Police, formed in the 1890's as protection for the settlers' Pioneer Column. Its name only changed much later, after Robert Mugabe became president, to the Zimbabwe Republic Police. I recently found in a trinket box a brass ceremonial cap badge, a memento of working in administration in its CID branch in Salisbury: a generously maned lion half stands, half crouches over a Zulu shield and several spears, while another spear seems to have pierced his shoulder. He is holding his head and tail improbably erect, his canine teeth clearly visible.

With Christmas approaching, whilst I was in what I hoped was the final stage of my pregnancy, Mark had been left with a double workload, covering for his boss's absence on long leave. Then came a fresh development:

You may have heard of the 'emergency' with troops being called out last weekend, with the NDP being banned (cheers) and all. This meant that all company staff had to do duty at the oil depot – they are all special policemen, only specifically to guard the depots which are 'key points'. Doug C [Fran's husband] had the midnight to 8 am shift, and Fran had gone into hospital for 10 days, which left the children alone, so of course Mark offered for us to have them. They were very good and seemed to amuse themselves and are terribly polite, ('Can I help you, Mrs. L-?' made me feel very OLD!)

***

The Nationalists' efforts at discouraging Africans from registering to vote, their looting, burning and violence in the townships, had driven the Prime Minister to call out the troops. Within a week of the NDP's banning, and despite the arrest of many of its leaders, a new organisation had been formed, the Zimbabwe African Peoples' Union (ZAPU), its aims and tactics the same as those of its predecessor. Joshua Nkomo, meanwhile, stayed abroad, seeking unsuccessfully to drum up international support for their cause, to pressure Britain to intervene and set in train majority rule. But there was much sympathy in Britain for the white cause, which no doubt contributed to the continuing sense among many of us whites that all would be well.

***

The closer Christmas got, the more I missed all the traditions of our large family get-togethers in dead of winter, the piles of presents that mounted on the big table on the landing, the dog-eared but much loved decorations we strung across the hall, the appearance of spare uncles and aunts, so that by the day itself we might easily be ten or more for Mum to cater for. Perversely I even started to miss the chill of a dark English winter day. Here in the hot sun that appeared between downpours, it felt ridiculous to be sweating over the stirring of a heavy Christmas pudding, or icing a fruit cake, though I did, unsure what to replace them with. I became set on making our first married Christmas as social as we could, and in an effort to settle in to the local community, we invited to drinks not only the few couples we could now call friends, but also some we hardly knew at all. Mark made an enormous and powerful wine cup, I laid on the nibbles – and alas, most of them simply did not come, citing when I phoned them vague and unconvincing excuses. I felt mortified, my pain more acute from having learned at boarding school the importance of being popular and in the thick of things, to stave off homesickness and isolation. Now, instead, I felt more lonely than ever. Of course in my letter home I didn't mention my feelings at all, just that the cup put the remaining few of us 'swiftly on our ears' and that after a huge scrambled egg at 9 we sent them reeling off into the night.

No health warnings for pregnant women in those days: I happily drank as much as everyone else – which was, by today's standards, quite heavily. Both beer – the local Castle and Lion lagers – and wine and spirits from South Africa were cheap. My favourite sundowner was brandy and ginger ale. Similarly, cigarettes cost little, made of course from local tobacco and all tasting much the same. We favoured State Express as being classier than Gold Leaf or Pall Mall, at around 1/10d for 30. At the budget end, for the African market, came Star at 2d. for eight.

The airmail service was surprisingly speedy in those days, and my letter wishing the family a happy Christmas was written on Sunday 17 December and posted next day:

I am sure you can easily believe that we would love to be there too, in fact were only saying so in wistful tones at breakfast this morning. Everyone here gets very homesick for snow, log fires and so on – carefully leaving out the smog and drizzle. We shall either boil and wish we could have fruit salad instead of plum pudding if only it didn't feel wrong, or be trapped by tropical downpours and wonder if we could manage at least the log fire bit after all.

In the event I need not have worried about loneliness, my post-Christmas letter giving a full account of our packed programme. We made the best we could of our limited budget, decorating the house with a small conifer felled from a vacant neighbouring plot and triumphantly conjuring homemade decorations for 10/-. We had also begun to get involved in Gwelo's only

Anglican church – we were both regular churchgoers then. It was an anchor of sorts in a new place, a way of entering the local community, and apart from the fact that the building was new, modern and light, felt little different to worship in from the parish church at home. I don't recall ever seeing a black face in the congregation. After much discussion about the risk of my fainting during a service, we opted to avoid the heat and go to Christmas Eve midnight mass (I sitting throughout near the door) – a wise decision as it turned out, because Christmas Day dawned cloudless and exceptionally hot. We opened the mountain of bulgy brown paper parcels with their green customs labels I had studiously avoided reading. Baby clothes mainly, for me, and a fine edition of Jane Austen's *Persuasion* from Pa, which I have to this day. There were records – LP's – of much missed classical music, a silk tie for Mark, and my mother, typically, had even remembered Daniel:

Daniel was thrilled with the shirt you sent, he said we must write and thank you but I am hoping to get him to write tonight, to enclose with this. We gave him a pair of brown canvas shoes and yellow socks which pleased him too. I don't think Christmas meant an awful lot to him, but he slaved on Christmas Day and then had all Boxing Day off, so was quite happy.

He did indeed manage the letter, respectfully written on a sheet of company notepad: [see next page].

(The expression 'smart shart' remained an affectionately remembered expression in my parents' household for years.)

***

It was not surprising that the limited education Daniel had received, and of which he was very proud, had been at a mission school. Successive white administrations had not considered educating the native to be a priority and had left it where it had started – with the missionaries. It took nearly 50 years for Rhodesia's administration to open the first state primary school for black children in 1944, followed four years later by the first secondary school. By 1950, according to Lord Blake's *A History of Rhodesia*, there were 12 government schools, compared to 2,232 mission and

Daniel. Son. of
MR. S. M. Lloyd

Dear madame thanks. Very much to given me. Hopping Xsimas. a Smart, smart. etc I dont think. Jean, forgeten you madame. and, I am very Grad. to. writing. that letter by to Say. Thanks my Grand mattar. But I carrying. to See you madame But I dont Know How can. I see. you. Eney. way the God. of. peace. be. with you all gird. By. madame.

Daniel

independent schools. Gradually this number grew; however, it was not until after independence that vocational colleges, polytechnics and other higher education establishments were developed in any number, to meet the great hunger for education, and the demands of industry for commercial and industrial qualifications.

***

By mid-morning on our first Christmas Day, I wrote home later, we were at one couple's for morning tea, another's for a cold lunch, and in the evening *after a siesta, Mark and I began preparing the dinner, which was quite a labour. We had turkey, ham and all the trimmings, with iced*

Vichyssoise first, and plum pudding with Mark's knockout brandy butter after
– a goodly evening with Fran and Doug, complete with cigars and liqueurs.
On Boxing Day we felt 'slightly decayed' but four other guests came for
morning tea, the men ending up playing cricket on the hard-baked lawn.
By evening we were celebrating the first rain for weeks, as we went out to
another couple's buffet supper.

It is a wonder all this did not bring me into labour, but it didn't. The
post-Christmas anti-climax came and I felt huge and clumsy, especially in
the heat. Naively I believed that my baby, officially due on 1 January,
would arrive on time, but 'Bert', as s/he was nicknamed, stayed comfortably
put. I became increasingly impatient, not convinced that this pregnancy
would ever end. In search of a change of scene, we took to going for drives:
a lovely drive to Selukwe in the afternoon, where there is a sudden change to
quite spectacular scenery. It isn't really a great treat for Mark to go driving at
weekends, but I hadn't seen anything round here except Gwelo itself – most of
the roads are so bad he won't take me anyway at the moment.

It is time I explained about the roads. Around town, and on the main
road between Bulawayo and Salisbury, you could rely on a fair width of
tarmac. Elsewhere it was very different, as my cousin John Watson, working
for Dunlop in the Central African Federation at the time, remembers:

'The roads were of several types. The most basic was simply a clearing
through the bush and, as the weather was mainly dry, the surface was dust
which got everywhere, up your nose, into your hair and clothes. Most frustrating
was to get behind a slow lorry which simply condemned you to driving in a
dust storm. To take a chance and overtake was to drive into the unknown and
for many an impatient soul this was the very last thing they did. The next type
of road was the 'strips'. These were narrow strips of tar, set apart approximately
the width of a vehicle's wheels. If nothing was coming, you were fairly
comfortable, but when another car came in sight you had to get the nearside
wheels off into the dust on the left. This was often quite a hazardous procedure,
but the Dunlop service engineer boasted that he had experimented with
differential tyre pressures and could go on and off the strips at 80 mph (the
speed limit was 50 mph). Next, there were the nine foot tar roads and now

and then you could find the luxury of a road where two cars could actually pass one another without driving into the dust.' He goes on to mention his *'brand new beige Wolseley 6/90, no mean barouche, well able to do the ton on the excellent stretch of new road south of Northern Rhodesia's Copperbelt'.* Later on, as he settled in, he could polish off the 200 miles in under three hours, to the astonishment of his friends at the Ndola Club.

In the midlands, things were slower: on the dirt roads we would pray for a road grader to have recently passed by, smoothing out the bone-shaking corrugations that had built up. Otherwise you had to try to achieve a speed that took your wheels surfing over the tops of them, to ease the ride. Mark's larger company Ford Zephyr had a better chance of this than our little old Morris Minor. Another real hazard was the open railway level crossings, with nothing but the engine's wail to warn you of an oncoming train – another frequent source of fatal accidents. It is no wonder that I used to worry whenever Mark was 'on the road'.

A strip road (with hitch hiker)

Eleven Spoons

On the sideboard, the canteen sits foursquare.
Silver forks and spoons nestle, each in its green baize bed, knives in the
lid. Daniel polishes them
once a week with the special cloth, along with
the silver teapot and the candlesticks.

The empty space gapes like a missing tooth
in a smile – eleven soup spoons. She checks
the kitchen drawers, the sink, the garbage bin,
runs to the compost heap and rummages through rotting vegetables. It
must be somewhere.

Daniel – she shows him the empty slot. Their landlady
had said *Keep everything locked, you can't trust them.*
Neighbours talk of marking levels on the Gordon's,
the sugar jar, of keeping tallies of tins. He's looking
startled, shakes his head, *No Madam, I don't know.*

*It must be somewhere, Daniel. If you know, you must
tell me.* She waits. He's sweating now, but still
he shakes his head, no. She makes him help her
search each room, the flower beds by the stoep,
the compost heap again, desperate for a glint.

Daniel follows her, hangdog, past rows of mealies,
cabbages, carrots that need thinning, a sprawling
pumpkin patch. She looks at the closed door
of his kaya, back at his sweaty face. His *No, Madam*
is urgent now, his eyes reproachful.

She stops. Above them, a turtle dove is purring
in a musasa tree. Absently she tugs at a straggling weed.
We have to keep looking, Daniel, it must turn up.
Back in the cool of the house she closes the drawer
on the empty slot, clicks the lid down.

CHAPTER 4

'Quite the most beautiful thing I'd ever seen in my life'

It is January 12th. I'm sitting on our shady stoep in my now well-worn sleeveless blue smock, my new friend Anne Smith beside me – beautiful, calm, reassuring Anne. She is holding her watch, saying 'Well done – you're down to 6 minutes between contractions now.' Yesterday, on edge from the long wait and the heat, I convinced myself I could feel labour pains, was admitted, but it came to nothing and I was sent ignominiously home. This time feels different and I know it is for real ...

Now I am in a small delivery room half-lying back on a high bed, my legs hoisted up in sort of stirrups, feeling tired from pushing, and the doctor – there are a lot of staff around – is saying something about my being too small, about forceps and anaesthetics. And even though I don't want this, I am going ...

And that's how, at the last, I missed our son Paul's arrival at 8.20 that evening. I woke to hear my baby's cries but to my intense disappointment *'he was whisked away to rest – and after the forceps they thought it would be better for me to see him all tidy.'* So Mark, who had called in to see how things were going (husbands being expected to stay well away from the birth) was first to see him, and then to reassure me of what a fine son we had. Then *'I was meant to sleep, but didn't manage very well, in spite of drugs etc. It was just that I was so excited to see my son and so thrilled altogether, I kept on waking up and smiling all by myself in the dark, till 5 a.m. when at last they brought him. Of course he was quite the most beautiful thing I'd ever seen in my life. I believe that in fact this wasn't just the maternal eye of love, but that he was fine looking as babies of that age go, since he had had only a short struggle into the world, so wasn't a bit wrinkled or red. Mr. D – made a fine job of the forceps and there is hardly a mark to show ... I just spend my time thinking how lovely he is!!*

Then began ten days in the mothers' ward, where our every moment was controlled by nurses and we lived in a strict four hourly routine. The high points were when the babies were brought to us, when I was allowed to hold my son, to nurse him, wind him, unwrap his swaddling shawl and admire his perfect fingernails and chubby clenching toes. I lived for those times, but all too soon, in a rustle of starched uniform, nurses would bear our babies away to a separate nursery. *'Of course whenever one of the babes in the nursery yells, everyone worries that it's theirs being hungry, but the nurses will never tell!'* We were given lessons in bathing and nappy changing, but great swathes of time had to be passed reading magazines, thankful for visiting times – an hour in the afternoons (for friends) and evenings (mainly fathers). Mark was allowed to go down the corridor and peer at his fine son through a window, then we would gloat at how clever we had been, and he would bring me news of the outside world – of how Daniel was managing at home and of his work trips.

Why did not we mothers rise up, rebel, march down the corridor and claim our babies for ourselves? Well, because of course it was the way things were done then, best for mother and baby, we were assured. We were good girls and did as we were told.

At last the longed-for moment when Paul (still called by his pre-birth nickname of Bert) and I could go home, although unsurprisingly the regime left us, as new parents, ill-prepared for it: *Daniel was on the step to greet us, and terribly thrilled to see the 'piccanin baas' [little master] – I'm not sure he's so thrilled now with all the nappy-washing! At this minute I even have a fire going with nappies airing on a horse, as it's drizzled all day, the drought broke while I was in the home, and now the garden is green and lush and full of weeds, and there's no sun to dry the washing. – well, can't have it all ways! Our little Bert is very sweet and it's lovely to have him at home, I wish you could see him, he has such a dear face.*

I had known as soon as we got home that I wanted the baby in our bedroom, in his carrycot beside my bed. But here was the problem: my job was home and baby, but Mark's was to go out and sell, to drive across his sales area making contacts, to nurture business relationships and write reports – this last being something he hated and made slow work of. He pointed out that he needed his sleep. So the baby went in his cot in the nursery, which suddenly felt a long way from our room – actually across a wide corridor and a landing that was large enough to serve as our dining room. I was worried I wouldn't be able to hear him cry (which of course I could, perfectly well). When he was asleep I would gaze at him in wonder at his beauty. But when, during the day, he went on crying even when he had been fed and changed, when I had checked his nappy for a pin that might have come open (Dr. Spock said I could, but that it wouldn't have) – then I felt scared and inadequate. The first time it happened, I can remember suddenly realising, with a sense of near panic, that it was all down to me now – no nurses, no having him whisked away so I could rest. And yet here too was the loveliest thing I had ever set eyes on, our precious baby. It was an emotional roller coaster I had not expected and my anxiety leaps off the pages of those early letters home:

At night he has been very good so far, only shouting at the right time, for food. I regret to say that most of the day he yells. This I think must be wind, but I've tried everything, even a hot water bottle to not much avail. Apparently it will do him no harm to scream, but it harms me considerably, gets on my nerves and I can't rest.

My new women friends rallied round of course, admiring him and assuring me over endless cups of tea that this was normal, but this only temporarily eased my distress at the baby's crying. Did I ever wish my mother was there to help me, not 6000 miles away? No, I am afraid I didn't, fearful that she would have taken over, like the nurses in the home. They had never revealed whether they did any supplementary feeding between the official ones, and so whether my milk supply was adequate. A Child Welfare Sister arrived, said perhaps he is hungry, lent me baby scales for one day to check what he was getting. Of course, despite the fact that on weekly weighings he was gaining an ounce a day, I immediately decided that his crying was indeed hunger. It was all too easy to lose confidence in my own milk production and to start to supplement with a bottle.

Yet in spite of my anxieties, it is the joy I remember most vividly. There were quiet moments, just him and me together in the small hours of the night, as I carefully changed his nappy, wondering at the perfection of him. I would sit feeding him close to the open window, with the smell of warm night air heavy with rain, wind him looking out on the bush-dark night. His head would drop heavy against my shoulder, and I would stroke the soft folds of his nape, breathing in his baby scent to the pulsing shrill of cicadas.

Our attempts to keep my parents briefed on their grandson's first few weeks were dogged with mishaps, reminding me how difficult it was in those days to keep in touch with far-off loved ones. The fastest option was a telegram, which would be phoned through to the recipient, then followed up with the tickertape strips pasted onto a form. So on 13 January they received 'Baby born last night Amanda and son both well' – any more would have been too expensive. A couple of days later I wrote a long letter which seems, untypically, to have taken over a week to reach them. Meanwhile my parents had sent a congratulatory telegram, but alas, no-one told us that they had also prepaid for our reply, so I responded with another (slow) letter. At last a phone call was organised: you had to book international calls to reserve your 'slot' on the wires so to speak, then sit and wait for the phone to ring and the operator to announce, 'You're through caller'. If you were cut off (which happened frequently) you must jiggle the phone hook to attract the operator's attention and get reconnected. It was still a huge thrill though, as I wrote on our first wedding anniversary, 4 February 1962: *Thank you so very much for telephoning, and I'm only sorry they kept cutting us off. Still it was lovely to hear your voices – amazing how they really sound like you at that distance … Oh dear, hearing you makes me wish we could see you all, and especially for you to see Bert, what fun it would be.*

At about this time we discovered the best way to ensure Paul settled for the night: Mark had to give evening film shows on the company's products in two local farming towns and rather than leave me behind, we stowed the carrycot on the back seat and set off along the dirt roads. As the car bucked along the corrugations, silence fell in the back, and I was able to leave him there peacefully asleep – creeping out from time to time to check on him – till we got home.

Soon we were packing for Mark's long leave of five weeks, which meant that we could visit his parents, who lived in Cape Town. I am astonished to read that we had contemplated driving the 1,000 or so miles – a journey of a full three days at least. True, in that part of the world we were all geared to driving huge distances without thinking too much of it, because you had to. But I think it also shows how little we had understood the demands and needs of a new baby. Although I was thankful that bottle feeding had helped to settle the baby and me into a quieter routine, it was hardly ideal for the much longer journey we were about to make. Mercifully we decided we could just afford the air fares, and leaving Bulawayo on a lunchtime plane, and with a two and a half hour stop over in Johannesburg, we arrived tired out at 9.30 that night.

I called Mark's parents Mother and Dad, as he did, for it would have seemed over-familiar for me to use their first names. Dad was a big man, portly now, with a booming bass voice that was to earn him the name of Boompapa with his grandchildren. He had spent his career with an international oil company, first in India, then Hong Kong, where, on a business trip to Manila, both Mark's parents were taken prisoner by the Japanese for four years. Finally, reunited with their two sons, who had been taken to Australia for safety, they were posted to South Africa, based in Cape Town. Mother was a small neat lady (woman doesn't seem a suitable term for her somehow) who was a perfect foil for her husband, and who, I came to learn later, knew how to deploy her strong will with great tact and skill. Throughout her husband's overseas career she had planned for their retirement back in England, in a pretty cottage somewhere. But when it came to it, all his continued business interests were in Cape Town, as were most of their friends, and so they had stayed, keeping their British passports and visiting England once a year. Mother had found her English cottage in the southern suburbs of Cape Town; it was painted black and white, with leaded paned windows, full of Ercol oak and floral chintz. The garden, shaded by oak trees, was tidied and watered by a garden boy, and the blue shadow of Devil's Peak (a shoulder of Table Mountain) was a reminder that this was Cape Town, not the Cotswolds. Indoors was the province of Lily, stout and capable in her royal blue overall and white apron, queen of the kitchen and senior member in Cape Town of her extended family, many of whom came there to work from the Eastern Cape. She lived in a servant's room built in my parents-in-laws' back yard, visiting the family in one of the 'locations' on her two half days off, one being Sunday after the roast beef and Yorkshire and the apple pie had been cooked, served and cleared away.

***

Lily's relatives came to the city to work, for there was no employment back in the rural so-called 'homelands'. But they could only stay if they could get and keep a permit to do so, for this was South Africa under apartheid – separateness – rigorously maintained as a way of life. Mark and I perceived it as far more draconian than the separateness of Southern Rhodesia, although in truth this may have been largely because it was so visible. 'Whites Only' signs designated everything from the best beaches to post office counters to park benches. But all this was what was often called 'petty apartheid'; less obvious to us but far more profound in its effects was the Group Areas Act, which designated where you might live according to your racial classification (itself hedged about with a raft of laws).

Under this system Lily had a permit to work in Cape Town, returning to her family home in the Eastern Cape only on her annual leave. This arrangement was precarious for blacks: if your permit was withdrawn for any reason – and that threat was ever present – then back to the 'homelands' you must go.

I am greatly oversimplifying this whole elaborate legislative edifice. Apartheid's tentacles spread into every crevice of your life for good or ill, and for us whites, it was a comfortable and privileged life indeed. So it was small wonder that the African National Congress had resorted to abandoning its policy of non-violence, forming a military wing, Umkhonto-we-Sizwe (Spear of the Nation). We did not know it then, but Nelson Mandela had, two months before our visit, slipped secretly out of South Africa in search of support from other African nations for the armed struggle which nationalists now saw as inevitable, all other means of negotiating with the government having been met by ever harsher legislation.

My parents-in-laws' life ran to a well organised routine, Dad with his business interests, a governor of the University of Cape Town, steward at one of the two racecourses, Mother running a tight ship with Lily and organising their social life. By Dad's Lazeeboy recliner lay Chambers Dictionary and a thesaurus for tackling crossword puzzles. Before lunch, Dad with his pipe and Mother with eyes narrowed against the smoke from her cigarette had a pink gin – 'Gordons, with a lot of ice,' Dad would boom at waiters – and in the evening 'Bells whisky with a little water, no ice!'. They both played a mean hand of bridge and had respectable golf handicaps.

It is often said that the Western Cape isn't truly Africa, and it's true that it has a quite different feel to it from the high expanses of savannah, the semi-deserts further north. With its long dry summers and almost all the rain falling over the temperate winter months, it has a Mediterranean climate. The bush has given way to the high, pointy mountain range over which the first settlers took their ox wagons, heading north: below, from Sir Lowry's Pass, is the gleaming curve of False Bay and the pointing finger of the Cape Peninsula. That summer, with the cool shade of the oak trees, the vivid blue of agapanthus flowers on their long stems rising above begonias and busy lizzies in Mother's garden, it did indeed feel as if we had flown to a different continent.

All this was pleasantly familiar to me from our pre-engagement visit, as we arrived exhausted with our baby, and oh! what a relief it was to share responsibility for the baby with Mark now he was on leave, and with an eager but tactful granny. Mark discovered accidentally that if put down on his front, Paul went instantly to sleep – a practice forbidden now as a possible cause of cot death, but a life-saver for us thereafter. Soon Paul – we had managed to stop calling him Bert – was into a well organised routine, sleeping in a borrowed pram under the oaks, cooed over by Lily and shown off to family friends. Delicious meals appeared only too regularly ('we shall neither of us lose weight' I half-complained in a letter home). Mark and I socialised with his old friends (two of them to be Paul's godfathers) and their wives. We even managed a little tennis and the odd nine holes of golf, for which I had no aptitude, but which, because Mark loved it, was a good way of spending time with him.

Paul was christened in Cape Town – a proper 'do' at St Thomas's church, where he slept soundly as streams of water were poured over his head by the vicar. Then: *'There was tea complete with lovely cake adorned with stork carrying hammock, and lots of Veuve Cliquot '55 (or was it '53?) which went down well. '* Gifts ranged from silver napkin rings (3) and a silver mug, to Winnie the Pooh and Beatrix Potter books.

Then, quite suddenly it felt, our lovely, reviving break was over: *'we felt most depressed to leave Cape Town, and didn't at all relish the idea of coming back here. We fitted in a final swim and golf before we left, but became quite melancholy. After a night's stopover in Bulawayo, showing off our growing son to friends, we drove up here yesterday afternoon, arriving in pouring rain as in Nov. to find Daniel all geared up and cheerful, and everything in order. A lot of veg. are coming on now, but we have to start planting winter flowers...* Then, as the reality of life in Gwelo sank in, a little cri de coeur: *'Mum, have I any winter clothes left with you, as I really must get geared up for the cold here which I dread, and have no vests or warm dresses etc... anything would be welcome.'*

Amongst the waiting post, including parcels of 'tiny and not so tiny garments' from friends in England, was the big baby book my mother had kept, first for me (the eldest) at one end, and then from the back for my first brother Will. I avidly compared Paul's progress with mine and Will's. The tiny photos I stuck in his book seem little better in quality than those of me in 1938/39 and scarcely more numerous, the first ones taken by his godfather Skip at the christening and only arriving in Gwelo in May. What a contrast to the blizzard of digital images instantly available to us nowadays after every important event! It must have been particularly hard for my parents, having to imagine their grandson with the aid of my, and my mother-in-law's letters.

With Paul growing apace, feeding and sleeping well, the household now got into a new, better ordered routine. On weekdays Mark was off early, either to the depot, or into 'the bundu' to visit farming customers, and often home late too, having stopped off at the club for 'a beer or three' on the way back. How I hated this – the uncertainty as I waited for his car's headlights up the drive, longing to have a bit of time for us together before the next feed. But it was also a time of enormously enjoying my baby and his development, writing regular reports home of his new skills (hand to mouth, a range of vocal exercises etc) and commented: *I said to Mark the other day, it sounds to me as if Paul is getting spoilt, and he said, Well whose fault is that? So. I fear I am a bit goofy about him, I just dig that toothless grin! Daniel says he is just like the Baas (fat!) and 'too clever and cheeky' which is v. complimentary.* Although I hated it when Mark was away, which was for at least a night most weeks, there were endless coffee mornings and tea parties with neighbouring mums, and long sessions at the sewing machine while the baby slept outside in his pram, well netted, under a tree. I made almost all of my and Paul's clothes from inexpensive cottons bought at Desai's store, along with curtains, pram sheets and table cloths. It all saved money and was one way I could contribute to our very limited budget.

Twice a week I would go into Gwelo to shop, leaving at eight so as to avoid the heat, since I had to take Paul in his carry cot. I went to Desai's with a list of everything from insect killer to zip fasteners plus all our groceries and Daniel's rations. Then on to the butcher for vast quantities of meat – enough for a daily meal for us, for Daniel and for the animals. No Rhodesian man felt he had eaten properly without a decent helping of meat, which guaranteed a thriving trade. But shopping in Gwelo was utilitarian at best and what with the baby and the hot car I was always glad to get home.

And there I learned to garden and to love it. The vegetable plot was Daniel's province, though I chose what he grew. By arrangement he got to share the proceeds and worked hard at it. Peppers, aubergines, tomatoes, root vegetables, spinach, salads, onions, Daniel's mealies (maize) – everything – in my memory at least – thrived. I wanted flowers and raised trays of seedlings, which, if they survived their first week after transplanting into the red soil, produced a riot of colour in no time. It was the same with herbaceous plants. I became friendly with a neighbour, Gill Orner, whose husband was something in the Department of Agriculture. They had two rumbustuous little boys, constantly quarrelling; perhaps they were after their mother's attention, for her real passion was her garden. Under her guidance, and with Daniel's labour for the heavy work, I created a long, deep herbaceous border, backed by a rough stone wall. Unpromising looking offcuts from Gill's stock soon grew to fill it with blazing canna lilies, six foot rudbeckias, spires of lupins at the back, then dahlias and annuals – larkspurs, a haze of white mignonette, campanulas, snapdragons … the thrill of it has stayed with me, leaving me with a lifelong eagerness to make a garden wherever I have lived.

In April 1962, with Paul three months old, my letters start to look forward keenly to a visit by my mother to see her first grandchild in a month's time. Then suddenly she wasn't coming after all. The official reason was the house move: my father was within a year of retiring from his civil service job in intelligence, and they had decided to sell our big Surrey house for an old vicarage in Cambridgeshire, which would need serious restoration work. But, sadly, there was more to her change of mind than that, as my letters reveal: *I see your point about the £240 [air fare] all spent on you, but on the other hand it does seem as if you will get a good price for the house now ... I keep thinking it would be such a pity for you to miss Paul as a baby, as he certainly won't be by the time we get home. Besides we wouldn't be able to make it at all if the family should accidentally increase before then – that is a subject one just touches wood about and hopes! It would be much less if you sailed via Cape Town, plus 3 days rail to here (at least you would see some of Africa that way, if not in luxury).* Then after lots of baby news, I end plaintively *'DO come!'* But she wouldn't relent and allow herself the trip. (The phrase 'touching wood' referred to the notorious unreliability of the old dutch cap for birth control. Although Mark and I had learned with interest about the new birth control pill from friends Skip and Ann in Cape Town, we were still suspicious of it, feeling that it interfered too much with the body's natural rhythm.)

My disappointment at Mum's change of mind was intense, but I coped with it by keeping busy, and making life as sociable as possible. I reported *'a lovely Easter not doing an awful lot'* – but going on to describe a whirl of church services (Paul left in the car under a shady tree), two tea parties, a couple for supper and bridge, and nine holes of golf on an already iron-hard course, leaving Paul with Anne, who lived nearby – oh, and *'lots of gardening and carpentering'*! Daniel was given a day off which he spent at a Jehovah's Witnesses meeting – dismissed by me as 'a new amusement, I fancy'. Weekends were always our best times as a couple, all the more appreciated after the loneliness of Mark's inevitable nights away from home, and now we had a new-found activity to add to gardening and my sewing, and another way of saving money. We took to renovating old furniture which I bought cheaply in town, stripping down and painting a nest of tables and a standard lamp. There are glimpses of these in small black and white photos, along with Mark's patent bookcases – planks of wood stacked on small piles of bricks, cemented for safety, length and height tailored to our library's needs. (These however were not great: I came to rely on parcels of Penguin classics chosen by my father, and thus he introduced me to many of his favourite novelists – Henry James, William Faulkner, Patrick White and others.) What we couldn't make or restore, we commissioned someone else to; a skilled carpenter at the depot made a fine cot.

Our social circle continued to grow, mainly couples with young children, always ready with support and advice, the mums with time for tea parties. Jack and Joy Crouch also lived down the road with two terribly well behaved little girls dressed in frocks smocked by Joy. Jack was a teacher in town but had also designed and built their house; they subscribed to 'Parents' magazine, which supplemented my well-worn Dr Spock, and Joy taught me the Stork margarine fool-proof recipe for Victoria sponge. Jack it was who put Mark's name forward to be a church warden at the Anglican church, where I teamed up with Joy on the tea-and-cake roster after morning service. The Crouches also had a tennis court, made out of dead anthills. Recipe: take the finely worked red earth from several abandoned anthills, spread it, roll it and stamp it down, water and leave to bake in the Rhodesian sun, them mark out your measurements. Despite the unpredictable ball bounces, it was a great resource. We saw a lot of the Smiths, Pete a tiny, vivid almost Toulouse-Lautrec-like figure, talented and artistic, Ann taller than he, statuesque, calm and beautiful. I much admired their bungalow, the interior of which they had magically transformed into something elegant and original, against which ours seemed very ordinary. I remember too a Polish bachelor colleague of Pete's, nameless now, always good for making up numbers at poker and pontoon. It turned out to be helpful too that I had met Kay McLoughlin in the nursing home where she had twins just before Paul's arrival (watching her juggle their demands made me feel positively calm and in control!). Kay's husband Alec was the local vet, and we had just acquired an Alsatian puppy, eventually – and boringly – called Boy. He was a gentle, biddable creature, but nervous, which made him difficult to train; he needed more patience than I had got for the task, and Mark was seldom free to give him the time it needed. Boy played endlessly with Twist the half Siamese kitten, who later when Paul was old enough to play on a rug, became a great favourite.

Daniel had now worked for us for over a year and I wrote home: *I daren't ask him if he wants his leave, what shall I do when he's away, polishing acres of red stone floor? Horreur …* My mother must have passed on this worry in her correspondence with Mark's mother, who, as an old hand at employing servants, wrote back reassuringly : *I'm sure Daniel will find a substitute when he goes on leave. They always do, and it seems to be a point of honour with them to find someone who will do the job properly and not let them down. But it is a nuisance to have to break in someone new who is not used to one's ways.*

I suppose it could be said that I had 'broken Daniel in'. More accurately, I think, he had learned to cope with my impatience and was good at soothing my short temper with many a 'yes madam' and 'no madam' in his soft voice. He was very fond of Paul, the 'piccanin baas', often pronouncing him approvingly as 'too clever' or 'growing too big'. He would push mashed vegetables or fruit through a sieve for Paul's lunch, just as I had watched as a child our cook Mrs Hoverington doing for my little brothers. I remember one occasion when some unfamiliar taste made Paul turn his head determinedly away in disgust. Daniel watched my mounting impatience as I vainly tried to push the spoon between his firmly clamped lips – 'Come on, just a bit!' – and his soft 'No, madam' instantly defused the situation as he hurried forward to offer a plate of mashed banana, Paul's favourite.

On the Back Road

The sun burns through her shirt, and she thinks
of the seedlings in her front border –
double petunias, rainbow zinnias, stocks
for evening perfume, of puddling them in
last night, and how each one shelters now
under its little paper hat, reminding her
of her father on the beach, beneath
his knotted handkerchief.

The pram bumps along the rain- gouged
ruts and potholes, joggling the baby into sleep.
A grader must have passed here years ago,
its steel blade smoothing the bulldozed earth,
leaving heaps of spoil for verges and a road
still waiting for new settlers' bungalows.

And there, where scrubby grasses spill
over the dusty track, a delicate flame lily
bobs in the wind, its flared orange petals
shouting at the sun.

CHAPTER 5

An unexpected visitor: of racism, language and locums

Out of the blue, a telegram from home, making nonsense of Mum's argument about unaffordable airfares, for it announced the imminent arrival of Simon, the middle of my three younger brothers. He was 18, waiting to go up to Oxford in the autumn and I suppose at a loose end. Now was his chance to 'see Africa', Mum thought, making a few trips around the country using us as a base. Perhaps he could get a temporary job to pay his way, though Mum's offer of £2 a week towards his keep was more than enough on our budget. We were delighted: for me it was the first direct family contact for 15 months, and for both of us a way of showing them our lovely son. We felt sure Simon could see plenty of the country by hitchhiking, though we were less optimistic of any paid work.

What excitement! There was just time for me to write suggesting that Simon catch the train from Salisbury: *it will be a suitable introduction to Rhodesia Railways, though the train will take him 9½ hours instead of 3½ by car.* He arrived hot and dusty, full of tales of the slowness of the train, and wonderment at the small crowds assembled wherever it stopped. I remember him saying incredulously '*they were just sitting – doing absolutely nothing*'. As well as bringing all the news of home – our parents' house move and attendant dramas – he bore, incredibly, a small package of carefully wrapped lilies of the valley, which arrived '*fresh and smelling gorgeous*' – such a powerful reminder of an English May. I am touched now, thinking of my mother gathering the little bouquet of her favourite flowers, packing it so carefully to keep it fresh, sending it to the daughter she couldn't allow herself to visit.

Mine were not the only letters home our mother kept; many of Simon's from that visit have survived, a bundle of bulging airmail envelopes plastered with small value stamps, and giving detailed accounts of his stay – detailed because, as he explains now, our parents had instructed him to tell them all about our life and of course their grandson. Some of his letters are even headed 'from your correspondent', the language heightened for amusement and excitement, as indeed mine was from time to time, for as both of us knew, Mum would be likely to share our news with all and sundry. She was a great correspondent within our large extended family, and I can also see her now, down the hill at Worsfolds Stores and Post Office, talking to Miss Bowles through the grill as she collected her family allowance. Miss Bowles had only to enquire '… and how are the children?' for Mum to pull from her well worn leather bag rustling airmail sheets to quote the latest accounts of our doings.

There is something guilt inducing about reading letters not intended for my eyes, even though I have been given them by their author. Serve you right, I say to myself, as I read what is, in parts, a very different account of our life from that of my own letters, let alone from the memories in my head. Some comments are simply surprising, others downright uncomfortable – reminiscent of the sudden unexpected view of one's body in a fitting room with angled mirrors, and thinking Goodness, do I really look like that? – only worse. I keep reminding myself that he was 17, I only 23, and it was all a long time ago. And after all, we were both writing from our own, very different, experience.

How happy I was at Simon's visit! We had a lot to catch up on when he arrived, and my loneliness, especially during the weeks when Mark was away, comes through in his descriptions of us endlessly talking over cups of tea, and of car journeys passing swiftly as we chatted all the way. There are early glimpses of Mark and me as a couple in Simon's letters home:

Amanda and Mark are very happy; they both work hard. Amanda is the same Amanda and Mark is Mark. Amanda talks a lot and Mark little. Amanda talks to me about everything – we spend a good deal of time over cups of tea; the biggest topic with her is Paul and baby theory in general – an inexhaustible subject and one that is new as well as interesting to me. Later on he comments: *Mark was placid as usual* [in the face of one of my outbursts of impatience]. He *deals very well with A's moods, either taking no notice or laughing and he's marvellously patient … she is terribly submissive, loving him as she does. The other day when she had forgotten to take the order into town, she said 'You must be so angry with me for being so stupid.' Mark of course couldn't care less and said words to that effect!*

He was delighted with the luxury of life with a live-in servant: *It's a long time since I've strolled into the dining room to a ready made breakfast and the biggest coffee cups you ever saw – v. pleasant. Mark goes for a run every morning!* He was less keen however on the way we dealt with Daniel: *If he forgets the butter he is talked to in very stern terms and warned what will happen to him next time. A and M say he would never remember anything if he wasn't shouted at and I'm beginning to see that perhaps this is so. … the blacks one has dealings with are generally servile and 'sir-ing' the whole time, Daniel especially – a thank-you from me produces three or four from him. This afternoon he came into the drawing room to say goodbye (he always says goodbye when he goes 50 yards down the garden to his kaya!); my reply of 'good afternoon Daniel' evoked 'yes, yes, yes master …mumble mumble…' and a hasty backward shuffling of feet out of the door.*

The letter is a sharp prod to my conscience, puncturing the balloon of my vague and comfortable illusion of having been a decent, benevolent employer. I can see young Amanda back in that dining room, noticing that there is no butter on the breakfast table. She is exasperated, has told Daniel so many times and yet he still forgets. 'Daniel!' she shouts, 'the butter!', scowls at him as he hurries in. It is the same whenever he forgets something he has been instructed, or fails to understand. She does not learn patience, feels no need to do so; after all there is no-one to hold her to account for her behaviour, which she would not consider racist. Even her husband would not criticise her, something which is very important in their relationship.

Yet suddenly I am remembering that it had not always been so – that when that 20 year old English girl had arrived in Africa back in 1959, she had behaved rather differently. In Lusaka, still new to her 'au pair' role, her cousin had sent her down to the labour office at the Boma to hire a replacement houseboy. In the shade around the edges of the large courtyard squatted dozens of men, hoping for work, their eyes seeming to follow her as she hurried into the employment office. She felt a worm of embarrassment, but at the same time an uncomfortable sense of power – her power over them, she with a job to offer, so many of them waiting. And shopping downtown one day, she had watched a sour-faced young white woman behind a counter responding to a hesitant black customer's *I want pencil* with a snarl of *You gotta say please or you don't get anything! Please, you hear? Don't you have any manners?* Sharply in her haughty English voice young Amanda had interjected: *How can he learn manners if you treat him like that?* The woman only glared uncomprehendingly. Later, living in Salisbury, she began to attend services at the Anglican church in one of the smarter suburbs, for she had been brought up to go to church regularly and still felt it was the right thing to do. One Sunday she listened to the vicar sermonising on the evils of universal suffrage, then being promoted by the British government: *In U.K., they don't have it! Criminals in prison don't, lunatics in asylums don't ... what they don't understand is that not everyone here is fit to have the vote!* She wanted to stand up, to denounce him as a racist, or at least to stomp out, muttering her disgust. But she did not – though she did not go back to that church. She was young and idealistic in a vague, un-thought-through sort of way, but also naïve, without the resources to argue a case in the face of the standard rebuttal of: 'You Brits just don't understand – it's different here'.

And, desperate as she was to fit in to this delightful new life, she had got the message: we have no truck with Britain and the Brits here – you must leave all that behind.

So yes, as that young woman, I had learned the terminology: black people were 'natives', 'blacks', 'munts' or – often in an abusive or otherwise denigratory tone – 'kaffirs'. Or, of course, as employees they were simply 'boys' or 'girls'. People of mixed racial origins were 'coloureds'. Simon's letters often refer to 'niggers', a term still in common use in Britain then, though I do not recall hearing it used in Rhodesia, even among recent immigrants. However, there was much that I had failed to learn about the people among whom I was living, indeed had not even attempted. Longer-term settlers, who with their blunt language and behaviour I would have perceived as less 'liberal' in their attitudes to black people, in fact engaged with them far more directly and personally, both in awareness of their culture and in learning their language(s). At the very least they would use the simple pidgin that had evolved between the races, first as Fanagalo in South Africa and later as Chilapalapa in the Rhodesias. It was often referred to as 'kitchen kaffir' and shared words from local Bantu languages with some English and Afrikaans thrown in.

Over sundowners and at braaivleis, I had already heard plenty of Rhodesian jokes, the point of which was to show how stupid the African was, usually because he had misunderstood the white man's English. Recalling one or two of these now serves to remind me of how often I judged a black person as unintelligent simply because they did not speak English sufficiently well for us to communicate effectively. There was no question of my learning their language, it never occurred to me to attempt it, for it was my assumption that they should speak mine. In this I suspect I was typical of the British immigrants who had settled in the country in their thousands during the 1950's, most with no experience of employing servants, let alone ones from a very different culture from their own (and for whom the Federal Government's leaflet, with its guidance on pay, accommodation and rations had been created). The fact of the matter was that in the midst of this very enjoyable white Rhodesian life, there was still something very foreign and disquieting about its African-ness, something of which I was barely aware at the time. In his *A History of Rhodesia* Robert Blake quotes Frank Clements's *Rhodesia: the course to collision*, describing among the British immigrants of the 1950's an insecurity, a vague unease, at the scale of Africa, the extremes of weather, and '*the ever present black faces, unreadable, exotic and separate, the high chattering incomprehensible voices [that] filled them with a sense of menace*'. Yes, I think now, that chimes with my memories – of how often I felt discomfited by the presence of so many, to me, inscrutable black faces. Easier to keep them at a distance than to engage with them. Better to shout and hope that they would understand my English.

Now here was my young brother in this strange new environment, telling it as he saw it, discomfited by my shouting at a shop assistant in Desai's, 'the store that has everything', as we attempted to buy him some canvas shoes: *She always shouts at niggers and I find it most embarrassing! Because I expect them to be annoyed or offended. They never seem to be and Amanda says that they're so unintelligent that they simply don't take any notice of what you're saying.*

My own everyday life being pretty uneventful, I had worried about how to amuse an 18 year old, and Mark bemoaned his inability to find any single (white) girls for him, our friends being all married couples. But Simon and I came from a family of do-ers, so it was easy for him to join Mark and me in our hard work. Soon he was clearing out old sheets of tin and asbestos around the property, helping Mark with one of his ingenious handyman projects, constructing a dog kennel out of found wood planks – *big enough to house a cow*, he wrote. Later he was roofing the hen house, and helping me make marmalade. And nephew Paul was good fun: '*Naturally he sleeps most of the day which is a bit boring, but he's usually good for a laugh when he's not; he thrashes around madly, clasps anything that comes to hand, be it uncle's finger or his nappy. When he was left alone this evening after his feed and before bed he howled until someone came to soothe him; when they did come he grinned wildly from ear to ear and flailed in all directions. Just bored, Amanda said! The dog is good sport when there isn't a*

Paul and Uncle Simon enjoying a quiet read (note beer mug and ash tray)

baby available. Yesterday we frolicked on the lawn (which is like coconut matting) and I tried to teach it to chase a ball – at the moment it takes one look and runs away as fast as it can, but I'm getting on well and it's a good learner.

Winter was now approaching and my letters home are full of thanks for parcels with sleeping bags for Paul and sweaters for us. Despite my complaints, winter was not really cold – a sweater in the evenings probably, a log fire if you had a chimney. More importantly, winter was the dry season and watering became a lengthy task, the lawn of tough kikuyu grass must be sprinkled at dusk, and all my little plants watered constantly. But our garden was not fenced and soon our relatively green oasis meant we were plagued by rabbits. While Simon was with us, we managed to borrow a shotgun from a neighbour and he would sit on the stoep at dusk with it, glass of wine to hand. I looked up 'how to skin a rabbit' in Mrs Beeton, and failing to find it, followed the instructions in my American *The Joy of*

Cooking together with helpful diagram (I should have watched more carefully when our mother dutifully 'dressed' the furred and feathered game our father brought home from his shooting expeditions, grumbling over the scullery sink. She always said hare was the worst – 'so bloody' she would shudder.) I remember how diverted Simon and I were by the instructions for preparing squirrel, with its diagrams of gloved hands grasping key parts of the creature, and feet in dainty lace-up ankle boots (the latter for holding down the tail while you pulled the skin off like a jersey). Forty years later, our local butcher tells me that grey squirrel is the ultimate in healthy, environmentally friendly meat – free range, plentiful, lean and organic!

An on-going theme throughout Simon's stay with us was the saga of Daniel's leave and its consequences for the household. I had been unable

Car washing on the dry lawn

to stave this off any longer and it was agreed Daniel would have a month's long leave to go home. Simon's reports on this, more vivid than my complaints, start soon after his arrival:

22 May: Daniel is going to Nyasaland at the end of the month to get a wife. He has tried to get one here but they cost money. In Nyasaland they are free. He says he will provide a substitute while he is away and this morning a woman came round to offer her services but, as Mark was away, she couldn't be engaged yet. She can do everything Daniel does except chop wood and (marvellous) she was once a sort of nurse and can therefore baby-sit. (By 'costing money' Simon was referring to the system of lobola, whereby payment is made to the family of the bride, in cash and/or in kind – often head of cattle).

28 May: Daniel has collected an African to take his place – a female called Maria (by us). They have been working together for a few days so that we hope she knows the ropes when Daniel goes on Weds. She has no English and can't cook so A is a bit apprehensive, but if she is trustworthy we can leave Paul with her when we go out. (Up until then, our only options had been to take him with us in his carrycot, and leave him with friends if we were going to a restaurant or the cinema).

So to my great trepidation life without Daniel began: *7 June: Maria is far from a boon (please apply to [Uncle] Paul and [Aunt] Bets for a description of her setting the breakfast table) and stank like a midden until Daniel told her to wash. Daniel departed in a big grin and as bashful as a maiden in his smart new clothes carrying a suitcase and enough blankets to keep warm all the refugees in Europe. Re Maria, he said 'If she doesn't work nice, madam, give her good hiding' – which of course is the way these African men treat their women.* (By the same post, I describe the departing Daniel as 'looking like Dr. Banda in his black homburg'.)

My understanding of Mark's job, of how he spent his working days, was hazy. I don't remember him talking much about it, probably glad to put it behind him. By the time he got home, often to a late supper, he would be greeted by a lonely wife, desperate for his company and secretly envious of, as I saw it, his freedom to be out socialising, whilst with Paul in his cot I had only myself for company. Even if I had been free to go with him 'on the road', I don't think it would have been considered proper. However, a visiting brother-in-law was another matter, and here is Simon's description of a day out with him:

We started at 7.30 and made for the bush, visiting a sawmill, a huge ranch that must have had about 55 million acres. The [private] drive was about 15 miles long and we hit our heads on the roof about once every 25 yards. The roads, once you get outside of town, are not tarred but are not uncomfortable at 50 miles an hour. We went to several gold mines and went down the shaft of one of them. When, however, the boss said that he thought they were about to begin blasting, you couldn't see Mark for gold-dust! We also visited a native reserve where there are 11 Europeans to 40 – 60,000 Africans – must drive them mad. We returned to Gwelo in the dark and had a well deserved drink at one of its numerous hotels; it's part of Mark's job to sit around in pubs because he can pick up many useful hints about people wanting petrol etc. Once there's a drink or two inside Mark his tongue is loosed; last night I could hardly stop him.

Simon took to all our friends, whose welcome ensured a non-stop social life during his visit: *They are all charming – unreserved, friendly and open. I like them very much,* he wrote. Perhaps he sensed too what had drawn me to life in Rhodesia from the first – the classlessness of it. We had been brought up in a home where everyone was judged along class lines: their accent, language, behaviour – all were scrutinised against the template so vividly described by the novelist Nancy Mitford as 'U' or 'non-U' (U standing for upper class). Whole swathes of vocabulary were 'out': settee, note paper, toilet, pardon … such words betrayed non-U origins. How ridiculous it seems today, and how gladly I had, as I thought, put it behind me as I mixed with people (white people of course) from very different backgrounds. In fact I had absorbed all that 'correct' vocabulary, those 'right' ways of doing things, and was happily oblivious to what my own accent and behaviour told others about me and my background. I had also, without realising it, left one class system behind, only to enter another one even more rigid, based on the colour of your skin.

Most of our Gwelo friends of that time were, I think, immigrants from

Britain, either recent or having kept their links with 'home'. They were also well educated, the husbands professionals or similar – Mike the schools inspector, Jack the teacher, Pete a designer for Bata, Mark's colleagues Doug and Noel, Alex the vet. (The wives of course were all homemakers, most of us with young children). Simon distinguished between our friends and people he called 'Rhodesians', people with the strong accent very like South African, with its echoes of Afrikaans, but also perhaps – in the context of his letters – less well educated. Here he is, describing our trip to Bulawayo where an old university friend of Mark's was captaining the British Lions in a rugger [sic] match against the Rhodesians:

On Saturday morning the four of us set off in the little Morris for Bulawayo. It's a 2½ hour journey – a hundred miles and deadly boring. We arrived at the Thompsons for a late lunch... then set off, just Mark, Amanda and myself, for Hartsfield. We had very good seats for which Mark paid: the game was quite good if one sided – the Lions won by 35 points to 6. The Rhodesians are a very rough lot – there were 6 injuries on the Lions' side and none on the Rhodesians'; one Lion got his leg broken with a noise that 'resounded like a rifle shot around the ground' according to the newspaper. While he was being attended to, the coarse Rhodesians who had gathered in numbers to see the game gave an unpleasant display of their rough character, by shouting 'take him off', 'leave him to the vultures', 'get on with the game' etc. etc. Amanda and I were in a fury over this and got very worked up, and I don't blame us... When we got home we changed and went out to dinner with the T.'s to a good restaurant, I wore my kilt to the surprise and amusement of my friends the Rhodesians; I'm afraid I don't like these Rhodesians; they have horrible short hair cuts and are very hearty and simple. They all look exactly alike and can be recognised a mile off (I shan't be having my hair cut in this country!). (Quite what Simon was doing with a kilt I cannot fathom, for we had no Scottish ancestry and it was hardly suitable attire for the sub-tropics.)

An invitation from our landlords, the Cummings's, gave us the chance for a trip to visit their new farm – little more than a smallholding really –

near Selukwe, some 30 miles away. I loved these drives away from dull Gwelo into the bush and the countryside here was hilly and green with trees, 'the horizons unimaginably vast' as Simon wrote. We found them down a very rough track, living quite happily it seemed, in very primitive conditions. Their house was constructed out of a sort of wattle and daub, of mud plastered over a wooden woven frame, with a thatched roof and stamped earth floor. Dividing interior 'walls' were no more than wooden stakes close together still awaiting some sort of coverage. With no mains services they were, like all country white folk, dependent on a generator and a borehole, their privy a long-drop in the little outhouse, or 'piccanin kaya' as it was called (p.k. for short). A clearing in the bush contained an enclosure for pigs and chickens and a substantial vegetable plot. I think now that we were all secretly shocked to see white people living so like Africans, but they seemed perfectly content and we marvelled at their determination and resourcefulness. Recently I was enchanted to find, in Doris Lessing's memoir *Going Home*, a lyrical description of her childhood home in Southern Rhodesia, a house that must have been built in much the same way. Lovingly she describes the frame of long tree poles, the mixing of mud from suitable ant heaps till the walls were covered in 'a sweet smelling mud-skin'; the roof thatched with long pale grass, and last the floor – more ant-worked earth mixed with fresh cow-dung wetted with fresh ox blood and water, stamped down and smoothed. To her the house was a living thing, responsive to the weather's moods, over the years becoming home too to small mammals, lizards and insects, occasionally a snake. Only the white ants posed a threat to the house's structure. As a child Lessing knew the geography of every inch of her bedroom's uneven, patched walls and floor, loved it too much to return years later to find out what had happened to it. We missed all of those possibilities, saw only a primitive and uncomfortable dwelling, driving thankfully back to our brick built, corrugated iron roofed homestead.

By the end of June we were eagerly awaiting Daniel's return and Maria had been 'let go' with some relief on my part – perhaps also on hers. Simon meanwhile made various touristic forays – to the Victoria Falls, to the great Kariba Dam on the Zambezi river, and to the beautiful Eastern Highlands, fetching up in Bulawayo visiting our cousins John and Toni, where he was press-ganged into helping with the decorating of their splendid bungalow and was given the visitors' tour of the local Dunlop tyre factory. With news of a live classical concert there, and encouraged by Mark, I drove down with Paul anchored in his carrycot (the carrycot however not anchored to anything), to join him and hear the visiting Stuttgart Chamber Orchestra. This was a rare treat for me, and with Paul safely installed with his little cousins Yvonne and Nigel, Simon and I had a night out, including after the concert 'a cuppa at a drive-in'. We are recognisable in the Bulawayo Chronicle's photo of the audience, sent home with an arrow pointing to 'Us!'. It reminds me of how much I missed music during those years, let alone live music; I was forever writing home with lists of classical LP's I would like for Christmas or birthday.

We drove home next afternoon to find no Daniel and, with Mark still at work, two hungry animals. Simon reported: *Daniel hasn't come back yet (it is now Sat.eve.) Maria quit a few days ago and I'm glad I'm here because A cannot be expected to do things like water the veg. garden, make fires as well as feed Paul and cook. Added to all this A. is suffering from a bad back – she says it is muscular – and both Mark and the doctor say she must take it easy for a couple of days so we all buckle to and get along v. satisfactorily. Mark thinks she ought to go to bed but she won't; if she has to, I am sure I can look after myself and Paul. As regards the latter there is nothing I can't do (tho' I must say the changing of nappies (the unveiling as A. and I call it) is a bit distasteful to me).*

Brave Simon, prepared to step so wholeheartedly into the breech! The 'bad back' was a weakness in our family, with my father frequently laid up with a slipped disc, and Granny once frozen into immobility over the sideboard as she carved a chicken. I had already, aged 19, had two prolapsed discs removed, so any recurrence would have felt traumatic. Nonetheless, despite all offers of help, I would have felt it quite wrong to rest – that would have been giving in to it.

All our friends now warned us that we had lost Daniel for ever (despite a promised bonus on his return of £6) – or joked that the Malawi freedom fighters had caught him. But on 4 July a letter arrived, announcing he had found a wife and would we please meet him from the train on Sunday 31st June. Had he meant last Sunday, 1 July, we wondered? But then why wasn't he here? All we could do was wait, but by 5 July he had not appeared.

Gloom descended again, and my back had had enough of running the house, even with Simon's support. It got horribly dirty and dusty as the dry season progressed, and I am sure none of us even attempted to polish those acres of red cement floor. It seemed to take all day for us to do little else but laundry, which must be washed by hand in a stone sink, the ironing (including both sides of every towelling nappy), cooking and attending to Paul. Mark and Simon chopped wood for the boiler, but who got up early to light it for those morning showers, I wonder? At any rate, there were no more leisurely elevenses over endless cups of tea for us. Simon, now comfortably used to being waited on, wrote to the parents : *it was ghastly – all that washing up etc and no time to call one's own.* With still no Daniel, and expecting a weekend visit from our Bulawayo friends the Thompsons, their three boys, grandma and nanny, I decided to take on a temporary replacement – or rather, in the event, three in succession. Down to the Labour Exchange in town we went, expecting to find plenty of candidates, since there were few jobs beyond the least skilled open to black people. Job segregation was applied on the same lines as in apartheid South Africa, so in those days, and with the benefits of accommodation and rations, domestic work was I think relatively popular. (This was to change in the 1980's, when democracy brought an explosion in job opportunities and of colleges offering vocational education and training, and domestic work became a lower status option, and hence the province of women. However, by 2008 rampant inflation in Mugabe's Zimbabwe meant its status had changed once again, as the cost of travelling to work could exceed the salary for the job, and it was a prized role once more, with its free accommodation, water, electricity and of course no unaffordable travel costs.)

However, for us in May 1962, there was a difficulty, as we discovered: we lived 6 miles out of town and few of the candidates were willing to come that far. The first one we managed to engage was, I wrote, *'no good'*, then there was *'quite a nice creature called Charlie'*; he however *'dropped all the silver onto the draining board from a height of a foot and when I reprimanded him, he sulked for hours'*. He was despatched, taking all Daniel's cooking utensils with him. Finally came Levi, who had a family and was desperate to acquire a good reference, in order to secure further employment. We drove him home, with his large wife, several children and baggage crammed into the Mini, and installed them in Daniel's kaya. Levi seemed competent and the relief in the household was palpable. To celebrate, we went out on the Friday night to gamble our small change at the Smiths', returning late to the complete surprise of being greeted by a delighted Daniel. I remember the moment clearly: he was *'absolutely worn out and covered in coal dust and beaming from ear to ear. He had come by train and got held up for a week at the border of P.E.A.* [Portuguese East Africa, now Mozambique] *for not having a smallpox inoculation, had to have it there and wait until it 'took'.'* Next morning we met his wife, a beautiful silent young woman who spoke no English, whose name – that is, her name for Europeans – was Inez. I improvised and gave her one of my dresses as a wedding present, and soon Daniel had her pressed into service at the washing line and in the vegetable patch in front of their kaya.

And so with sighs of relief, we could return to domestic normality. The Thompsons' weekend visit passed easily enough, with Levi kept on for the weekend to help, so that madam, much relieved, wrote home *'it became more a question of direction rather than labour'*. Daniel and his new wife, however, were spending their first nights in his kaya in the company of a strange couple and their several children.

Daniel's absence had made me infinitely more appreciative of him; I would like to think that it also made me a better 'madam', more tolerant of his memory lapses, kinder to him when my own insecurities tipped me into ill temper, but I cannot be sure of that.

In late July Simon returned for the last time from one of his sight seeing trips and his final departure was looming. In his last week with us his letter records six evenings out of seven spent either in town – his thank-you dinner for us, the cinema for Ben Hur – or at dinner parties to say farewell. Our friends had enjoyed his company, found him very sophisticated for an 18 year old and treated him as an adult, my mother when he got home commenting on how much he seemed to have grown up. He had also assiduously worked at mimicking a Rhodesian accent, with its squeezed vowels and many a 'Ja' and 'Ag men!' My last fling with him was to drive him to Salisbury to catch his Comet, leaving Paul with the Crouches for a night, and staying over with my old CID friend and colleague Barbara Yates. I felt miserable seeing him off, looking longingly at the sleek new Comet on the tarmac, set for England. Barbara cheered me up by absconding from the CID and we 'did the town', buying much needed lengths of material and shirts for Mark: *I got some super material and have made myself sage green linen-Dacron slacks and gingham Dacron over blouse to match, v. smooth. But the best thing was just to see all the fashions and shops, to spur me on to make an effort. One gets into a fearful rut here and I found I wasn't bothering.* Despite all our friends and our lovely homestead, Gwelo never felt anything other than second best to me.

CHAPTER 6

The sudden intrusion of politics and an election shock

The centre of my life though were my husband and my baby, his development an endless source of fascination and pride. I was now keeping a baby book, recording clinic weighings, additions to his diet, his vocal explorations (squeaks and shrieks) and physical prowess, soon to include his first crawling, backwards off the carpet. As he grew so, slowly, did my confidence as a mother. I stuck in what few little black and white photos we had, sending others, along with regular proud reports of all this progress to his grandparents, together with descriptions of him gnawing on a drumstick and on a piece of biltong (dried meat) given him by the butcher. He was on diluted evaporated milk, I wrote, since '*until the rains come there is no goodness in the cows' milk*'. I couldn't wait to show him to his grannies – Mother, who was coming up in a couple of months' time, and Mum, who had at last decided to visit us the following year, sailing to Cape Town and thence onwards by plane.

Daniel meanwhile seemed happy with his new wife, indeed had started to oversleep, much to Mark's rage as it meant no boiler lit and a cold morning shower. I bought Daniel a large tinny alarm clock, which helped most of the time. Inez padded silently about, helping her husband with the endless laundry, hoeing between rows of vegetables. You could see he was proud of her, though in front of us he would speak sharply to her, to show who was boss. On Daniel's afternoons off they would go out, Inez often wearing the dress I had given her. And on Sunday afternoons they would go to church somewhere, he in his suit and homburg hat, she in a frock with a white hat and gloves, walking off down the hot dusty track.

I remember watching Inez as she settled in, walking in that slow, stately African fashion, so different from my own hurried pace, back to her kaya. She is wearing a pink overall that hides her shape, but even so you can see that she is beautiful. She pauses by the baby's pram parked in the shade of a cluster of spindly musasa trees and peers in, and suddenly I think: She'll be next. With Paul awake more of the time, I have started to entrust her with taking him in his pram for little walks in the afternoon, and I am planning to teach her how to feed him his tea while I cook our supper, or make mulberry jam from the big old tree at the back, or run up a romper suit on the sewing machine. I try to coax her to use a few English words – baby, pram, nappy – but she is very shy. We pay her a pound or two a month – a fraction anyway of Daniel's wage for much more skilled work.

At about this time I acquired – I cannot recall how, but it must have been through Mark's business network – a nice little temporary part-time job. The Midland Show was approaching, the big event in Gwelo's calendar, and I was engaged by one of the tobacco companies to hover around at their various events and offer cigarettes to the visiting farmers, all for the princely sum of £2/10/- per hour, which was riches indeed to me. What a contrast between this casual rate for me as a white worker and the going rate for our domestic servants! Job reservation meant that the market forces determining 'white' and 'black' occupations were entirely separate and unrelated. I did not feel the least bit guilty about it, in fact I doubt whether I made the connection – it was just the way things were.

I was in my element, finding this new role quite easy, a little like passing the nibbles at my parents' cocktail parties: *On Thursday I started my new job, in the Members Enclosure before lunch. I wore my white linen dress (straight) plus State Express yellow sash, and held a silver salver with cigs and a gas lighter! It was quite a success, and all the farmers in for their one treat of the year were thrilled. It was very good weather. Friday was hectic, and Joy took Paul over for nearly all the day. I had a hairdo, spent lunchtime working, had lunch with Mark in the Enclosure (he spent a lot of time at the Show of course), a Sundowner party 5 – 6 working, and then the Arkwrights and Orners to supper before the Show Ball! Amazingly enough all went well, I had a fabulous hairdo which carried me through the day, and had everything organised beforehand. The Ball was good fun, we had a good table and a nice party, and the Salisbury Police Band were really hep man – we were all twisting madly by 1 a.m.!*

How I wish I had a photo of the cigarette girl! The white linen dress has vanished from my memory, but I remember the hairdo: my over-bleached hair (supposedly highlighted) newly permed, firmly sprayed and lasting without a strand out of place till the small hours. (My parents' birthday cheque had bought me *'a very superior hairdryer with a stand and hood like a huge bath cap, so one sits effortlessly as at the hairdresser'*.)

Then Mark was summoned to Salisbury for a residential course of a full fortnight, pitching me into a state of high anxiety. How was I to manage on my own for so long? My fragile confidence evaporated, for I was still very dependent on his steadying presence. It must have been this sort of situation, together with the constant travelling required of a junior rep., that Mark's parents had had in mind when they had urged us to postpone our marriage until he was in a more established position. But of course we had refused. Little Paul was recovering from a gastric bug, and by the time Mark set off on the Sunday I had gastric problems of my own, which nothing but the odd sip of brandy seemed to shift. Our kindly young G.P., after laboratory tests proved negative, advised me that my trouble was just *'nerves, worry and tension'*. Don't allow this to become a habit, he said, the odd nip of calming brandy won't hurt, so thus fortified I set off to join Mark in Salisbury for the weekend as planned.

The drive, although not that long, felt arduous and a little scary to me

Paul's first haircut

on my own, with long stretches of nothing but bush to either side and almost no traffic. (I am amused now to see how my fears contrast with Doris Lessing's enjoyment of a similar drive. Having been born and brought up in rural Rhodesia, in her memoir *Going Home* she describes stopping the car to go off into the bush and sit under a tree for the pleasure of being alone there.) But as well as being reunited with Mark, who was free for parts of the weekend, Salisbury meant meeting up with old friends, and going shopping with the little spending money from my work, allowing me to splash out on a white handbag and white court shoes. And according to my letters, another treat was the television, such a thrill in fact that it formed part of the social scene, with friends coming round '*to supper and telly*' with our hosts the Cochranes. Sally was a hairdresser and gave Paul his first 'hair cut' – in reality just a trim of the wispy bits, so he looked '*like a real boy*'. I spun out my visit until the Tuesday morning, getting home, I wrote, '*to find the house open, Daniel vanished and very little work done. Still, that's the way they are, you just have to be on their tails all the time.'*

No doubt I was, because in mid-September, with the cooler dry winter months giving way to warmth, I was working like mad to make everything nice for a visit from Mother, who flew up from Cape Town for a fortnight (Dad being too busy with board meetings to come). What an easy mother-in-law she was, undemanding, admiring, happy to busy herself with her grandson, playing with him with the toys she had brought. She helped me in the garden too, planting out dahlias and tending my roses – what thirsty plants I chose for that driest and hottest of seasons, whilst spurning pretty cosmos which flowered along the roadsides as a garden escape. We went to the baby clinic and out to innumerable tea parties; she even took our rather neglected young Alsatian in hand, buying him a brush to groom him of his moult. On 20th September we were busy with preparations for a drinks party we were to give in her honour the following evening. Mother was doing amazing arrangements with sheaves of flowers from my new borders, I making little sausage rolls, when the phone rang, and our domestic peace was interrupted.

As far back as May, Mother had written to my Mum: *I can't help worrying about them in Rhodesia can you? If there were any real trouble Amanda and Paul could get down to us quickly. Mark I expect would have to stay on the job. But I don't think it will come to that and don't lets anticipate it.* No mention in any of my letters during those months of any 'troubles'. But today's caller announced herself as the local W.V.S. organiser, phoning to ask if I had got our emergency bags packed? Had I laid in tins of food, candles, a supply of water in containers? I had not, I said, feeling rather foolish, for I had put from my mind any real sense of an impending crisis, despite rumours in town of people getting ready to leave in a hurry. Soon Mark called from the oil depot with the news that Z.A.P.U. (Zimbabwe African People's Union) had been banned overnight, resulting in a security alert. I wrote to my parents: *You should know ZAPU – Simon must know – the African extremists' party which took over from the NDP banned last year;*

Paul with his Cape Town Granny

everyone is delighted, as they have been terrorising, intimidating, burning and riot-rousing. People were worried not so much by that as by Europeans being driven to retaliate – much more dangerous! Anyway, enough of politics, because nothing is going to happen here, but I imagined your papers might have been mentioning 'incidents'. Mother says she is a Jonah and is always arriving in places as political troubles start!

I wonder now how reassured my parents were by my breezy overview of the situation, including my casual reframe, suggesting that retaliation by Europeans posed more of a threat than ZAPU-led violence. In any case I was far too preoccupied to heed the WVS lady's urging and buy in supplies, for our big drinks party must go ahead the next day, which indeed it did, with 24 friends to meet Mother, and Mark dispensing drinks on the stoep. Mother's flower arrangements drew much admiration.

***

By mid-1962 ZAPU were tired of negotiation, which had yielded nothing but this compromise of a constitution and the prospect of 'racial partnership'. They wanted confrontation and they wanted democracy to mean one man, one vote. So with Joshua Nkomo still on his travels abroad trying to drum up support, ZAPU activists had continued to lead a campaign aimed at discouraging blacks from registering to vote at the end of the year, and at general destabilisation of white rule. Hence their campaign of violence that had spread to white targets, with the threatened prospect of retaliation.

White Rhodesians meanwhile were getting much more windy than my letters conveyed. The prospect of black rule alarmed even the most liberal. Just north of the now fragmenting Federation of Rhodesia and

Our little family, including Boy and Twist (note new flower border)

Nyasaland, the Belgian Congo had in 1960, with no preparation or necessary infrastructure, been abruptly declared independent, and what had unfolded there was vivid in the minds of white Rhodesians. To say that the country had been ill-prepared for self-government was an understatement. There were no Congolese doctors, or army officers; only a handful of children had completed secondary education; there were only 30 university graduates – though 600 priests. But it was a land rich in mineral wealth, resulting in a scramble for power involving western powers as well as local rivalries. The inevitable result had been almost immediate violence, and the ensuing chaos had led whites to flee. My cousin John, who had been posted to Lusaka at the time, remembers the scenes: *Having commandeered anything with wheels – cars, lorries, ambulances, fire engines and other vehicles, they came pouring into Lusaka, where a depot with essential supplies of clothing and other necessaries was hurriedly set up. (This was the sad start of the Congo's slide, with its enormous natural mineral wealth, into years and years of civil war and holocaust).*

These scenes were vivid in the minds of white settlers all over southern Africa, and this, together with the economic downturn and rapidly falling confidence, meant that it was hard for Sir Edgar Whitehead to sell his United Federal Party's policies aimed at developing a black, educated middle class and at gradual multiracial power sharing. His party, he was promising, would repeal discriminatory laws, including most importantly the Land Apportionment Act, which kept the black population in over-populated, over-grazed tribal trust lands, and in locations outside towns and cities – a proposal greeted with horror by many white people. Nor, in the face of ZAPU's campaign, was he having much success in getting qualifying blacks to register as voters.

Much more attractive to many whites was a newly formed right wing party called the Rhodesian Front. Their policies were far more straightforward: what was needed now was stability and the status quo, with whites retaining total control, under which most blacks would be better off anyway. Continued 'separate development' would allow Africans gradually to learn the ways of democratic government, over many generations, under the guiding hand of the white man. This new party was led by three men most of us had never heard of: Winston Field, Clifford Dupont and Ian Smith.

***

The only other mention my letters made of the 'troubles' at that time was a few days later: *We thought ZAPU was upon us last night as Boy was barking furiously at 3 a.m. which he has only done once before – bark I mean – but we were still here this morning. Things seem to be pretty quiet now, but the army and police reserve are still out, so Mark didn't go away for the night as he had planned... PS Paul's 5th tooth is through, top centre, v. big!*

Maybe my casual way of writing about the situation was intended to calm my parents' fears, but I cannot remember ever feeling really scared. Whilst the images of whites fleeing the Congo remained vivid in my mind, I believe I still had absolute faith in the authorities to keep order, reinforced by that sense of invincibility of the young. By November we must have felt things were back to normal, for I wrote of Mark having been away for the entire week. Whitehead's United Federal Party held its pre-election congress with a goodly proportion of black delegates and, despite the low numbers of blacks registering to vote, he seemed to believe he was getting his message across. October, known as 'suicide month' with its relentless dry heat and a sense that the rains would never come, dragged on; huge clouds built up, only to dissolve into a white-blue sky. But in November the breaking rains – just showers at first, then drenching downpours – at last broke the long dry spell. Green suddenly sprouted everywhere, the land was tillable, Daniel planted his maize seed and both he and I were released from the endless work of watering. All around our homestead, the musasa trees, without any appreciable leaf fall that I had noticed, suddenly burst into their fresh spring russet, giving them a strangely autumnal appearance. Perversely, that was sometimes what I longed for – a cool, misty autumn day with the smell of decaying leaves and bonfires and a nip in the air.

The state of emergency ended and our social life got back on track: the

Smiths held a beatnik party where we all wore black and bopped till the early hours. Mother was promising to send me hipster pants for Christmas, and I was busy making the cake, mincemeat and other goodies so unsuitable in that climate. In a nod to events in the outside world, I wrote in November: '*What price Cuba eh? I daren't listen to the news these days.*' We seldom bought a newspaper, and although the Rhodesian Broadcasting service relayed a fair amount of British and some world news, it all seemed very far away.

As the pace of electioneering hotted up, even Mark and I, who did not qualify to vote, decided we should attend a hustings. We believed that Whitehead's United Federal Party had the right answers, and went to hear him put them forward. For some reason that meeting remains one of my most vivid memories of the time. We were at the back of the hall, so that I could pop out and check on Paul, asleep in his carrycot in the car, sitting among a number of black people, with most of the white audience at the front. There on the brightly lit platform stood this mild mannered, bespectacled man, holding only a few notes, his voice quiet and reasonable, as if giving a lecture on politics to a class of students who he was certain would get the point of what he was saying. But in front of him, as he must have expected when he came to Gwelo, were ranged the solid figures of white farmers from this agricultural heartland. Whitehead came across as sincere – I just kept wishing he would do a more assertive job of selling his vision. But as the consequences of his plan became clear to his listeners, the atmosphere became heated. It was said that he was deaf, but his questioners made sure he heard them. I remember a farmer, stocky and tanned in his khaki drill, rising to demand: *Are you telling me that this would end up meaning that my wife would have to sit next to a black woman at the hairdressers?* And he didn't like the answer, which of course was that, ultimately, yes, she would. Someone asked: *And how long do you expect it to be, before we get to this stage, of racial equality in government?* Perhaps fifteen years, was Whitehead's reply, perhaps longer. As the front of the hall erupted into indignation, I suddenly noticed two young black men sitting just in front of us, shaking their heads; one turned to the other, saying with quiet vehemence: *That's too long, too long.*

On 14 December came the elections. I remember well our astonishment at the result, which Martin Meredith in *The Past is Another Country* called '*a shattering defeat for moderation*'. The Rhodesian Front had gained 35 of the 50 white seats, Whitehead's U.F.P. was left with 15 white seats and the support of 14 African MPs who between them attracted a total of only 1,870 votes. We were stunned: this new, unknown little party had seized power, on a manifesto that made clear power was to remain in the hands of white people for the foreseeable future.

As the dust settled, for once Mark and I scanned the newspapers: there came a realisation that many of the Africans who had registered to vote – and they were only a small proportion of those who qualified – had simply abstained. If only a few thousand more had turned out, it could have been victory for Whitehead's United Federal Party. As it was, the Rhodesian Front would go on to run Southern Rhodesia its way for another seventeen years. Its determination that white rule would be preserved at all costs was to lead within a few years to bitter conflict and bloodshed, before Robert Mugabe's ZAPU finally led the country into independence in 1980.

The general mood among local whites, particularly the farming community, was delight, ours was gloom, but Christmas rescued us. We spent the long holiday weekend in Bulawayo staying with the Thompsons, driving down in our newly acquired little pale blue Mini estate car with its timber trim. On dirt roads it bounced and rattled horrendously, but fortunately the main road was metalled, for the Mini was laden with everything from buckets of flowers and festive food to our Christmas gifts from England, the rear portion taken up with Paul 'leaping around in his cage'. Now almost walking, Paul loved nothing better than to be with the Thompsons' three little boys and their stock of toys – mainly cars. I can still see him with a dinky car clutched in his little fat fist, learning to roll it along the floor with earnest *brrmm-brrmm* noises. And their Nanny was never far away and seemed seldom to be off duty, allowing us the treat of a frenetic social whirl. We twisted till midnight at a party ('*me in my little black*'), caught up with friends at endless coffee, tea and drinks parties, joined Mark's colleagues and their families for the children's party and an evening braaivleis. The rains had well and truly broken and on Christmas morning we hurried through drenching rain and mud to early Holy Communion before helping the little boys tackle a mountain of parcels. And of course we had the full, heavy, unsuitable Christmas dinner: *a 12lb turkey, a ham done in pineapple we had brought and my Christmas pudding (delicious!) with Mark's brandy butter.* Then, with Drambuie and Cherry Heering in hand, and no doubt with dyspepsia setting in, '*we saw the old Queen* [she was 36 at the time] *on telly, but thought her ghastly, grim and stupid talk about the wretched commonwealth as if it was really a heaven on earth which no one here thinks it is, and she never smiled once.*' We returned to Gwelo reluctantly, feeling very flat, but greeted by excited animals and a cheery Daniel who, despite my intermittent grumbles, had done as expected, feeding Boy and Twist, mowing the lawn and keeping our homestead secure.

I looked at our home with new eyes now though, for a conversation with the General Manager at the company's braaivleis had left Mark and me in no doubt that our lives were soon to change radically.

CHAPTER 7

A post-Christmas bombshell; of visits and farewells

Regardless of any political crises or developments, there was always a lot of speculation in the company about where you might be sent next. You had no say, but hoped that your next posting would be a step up – a larger sales area, a spell at a branch office or ultimately to head office. The company spanned both Southern and Northern Rhodesia; colleagues joked with Mark that so far he had been posted to smaller and smaller places – from Salisbury to Bulawayo to Gwelo – so where smaller from here? Watch out, they joked, you might land up in Mpulungu! This was the company's remotest posting, at the northern-most tip of Northern Rhodesia. Very funny, we said, thanks but no thanks.

Now my post-Christmas letter to my parents ended with: *You had better take a breath and sit down, because our latest bombshell is that we are being transferred again, sometime in the middle of next year. We shall only have been in Gwelo 18 months at most. It is hardly any use telling you where we are going, because it is the farthest flung post in the whole of the company's Rhodesian operation and 400 miles even from a railway. Abercorn in N. Rhodesia. If you haul out an atlas, it is on the bottom tip of Lake Tanganyika, surrounded by Congo, Tanganyika and Nyasaland, in fact by hordes of black men. There is one company man there, covering a vast area, and also for the depot on the lake shore at Mpulungu, the place actually on the lake. Abercorn is 22 miles and 2,500 feet up in the hills. Mr Whitehead dropped this bomb at the braaivleis, unofficially, and we await confirmation... there is no doubt it is a good thing for Mark, as he is so very much on his own there with a lot of responsibility, and they said not more than 2 years. From what we can gather from the rare people who know anything about the place, it is beautiful country, lovely climate (strawberries all year round etc and no winter) but the town is horrible with 3 European shops and 200 people* [I meant white people] *at most, but a nice club and a small lake nearby which is bilharzia free for bathing and sailing. I doubt if we shall find out more than that till we get there. Certainly we shall be better off, with a raise, NR cost of living allowance and nearly all your rent paid if not a company house. But no cinema, doing all your shopping by post, no nice hairdo's etc etc spring to mind. However we shall just have to make the most of its advantages. As soon as we know more about it all I will tell you, in the meantime you now know as much as we do, and more if you have a decent atlas!*

Reflecting on it now, I am sure that the news overshadowed the rest of our time in Gwelo. I remember feeling pleased for Mark at his promotion, but deep down I was also very scared. I had studied the map in our Readers Digest atlas, seen how far north Abercorn was, how close to the Congo, whose southern province, Katanga, ran like a finger alongside Northern Rhodesia's Copper Belt. The canny Belgians had insisted, back when international boundaries were arbitrarily drawn through local people's tribal lands, on their share of the area's vast resources of copper and cobalt. And the Congo was now, as we all knew, sliding into 'a cauldron of chaos, fear and violence', as Martin Meredith describes in '*The State of Africa*'. So I had visions of hardship and loneliness ahead in a remote outpost – and yes, of being *surrounded by hordes of black men*.

Happily though, we had two visits to look forward to before then to keep my mind off things – first from Mark's brother and his family, and then from my mother. And as if in anticipation of her trip, my mother seems to have kept no more letters from Gwelo, apart from one to Cape Town, welcoming her to Africa, but it is a time I remember well. Life had

With Mark's brother John and his wife Pat, Sam and Debbie

its steady hum of routine, Mark settled in his job, I with my network of women friends, and Paul such fun as he grew apace – first teeth, first words, first crawling, all recorded in his book. He was now moving around at speed, often on one knee and one foot, his favourite time garden watering, getting under the lawn sprinkler or pressing his hands into the muddy red loam around my newly watered zinnias and petunias. I was thankful for Inez, now earning her £1 a month taking him for walks; I am sure she would have preferred to strap him on her back, rather than rattle his cheap pushchair over the stony tracks as instructed. Once, absorbed in sewing a romper suit, I suddenly realised how late it had got. Usually Inez would appear quietly in the doorway with Paul on her hip, but now there was no sign, either in the garden or on the back road. No answer from Daniel either. I hurried towards his kaya, turned a corner and there were Inez and Paul sitting under a musasa tree. She was singing to

Paul: Look no hands Mum!

him and they were playing a sort of pat-a-cake. They looked up: *Mama,* Paul said and went on playing, while I, perversely, wanted him to have missed me. Inez was as slim as ever, I noticed, with no sign of pregnancy.

Mark's brother John, his wife Pat and their Sam and Debbie, aged about three and two, were on their way back to his job in Nigeria with another oil company, after Christmas in Cape Town. Suddenly toys and bricks covered the stoep and dinky cars were earnestly pushed back and forth. Our stone floors were busy with little running feet; Paul sat watching them for a while as they sped past, then, as if realising that all fours was no longer enough, let go of the bars of his pen and walked. It was a fun time, marred only by strangely cool weather, and all the more precious for not knowing how long it might be before we were together again.

Soon Mum was on the Pendennis Castle from Southampton, from where, true to form – for correspondence was meat and drink to her – she posted us a letter to reach us before she landed in Cape Town. I still have her

little pigskin writing case bought for the trip, with a small blotter and pockets
in the lid for envelopes and stamps, a ragged Union Castle label still tied to its
handle. I was in a whirl of getting everything ready for her, wanting to
impress; our landlords helped by sending a team of labourers to whitewash
the house and tidy up the grounds, so that all looked spick and span for
Mum – though mainly because they now wanted to sell the property when
we left. Before she arrived, we went down to Bulawayo for Mark to be briefed
on his transfer, now scheduled for 17 June, and to do some shopping, *for it is
quite awful how much we are going to need to take with us – more furniture etc.*

So in March 1963, having left Paul with Joy down the road, my mother
met her first grandchild sleepily lifted from his cot one evening; he was 14
months old. And suddenly Mum was a visitor in my home – a strange
turnabout for both of us. I had found it hard to imagine this, to picture her
sitting on the sofa, being waited on as a guest. Growing up, we had all
experienced our mother as constantly busy – running the home, yes, but
also involved with the Mothers' Union, the Young Wives, and endlessly on
the phone. We all longed, I think, to get past that air of preoccupation that
seemed to prevent her from giving us her full attention. Now here she was
with none of those demands on her time – how would that feel, for both of
us, I wondered. In practice, however, she joined me in my own busy-ness,
helping around the house but above all taking over her grandson, teaching
him to use a spoon properly, encouraging his walking. She even insisted on
more enthusiastic potty training, for in her day this would often be complete
by one year, being part of the now infamously strict and rigid Truby King
regime of baby rearing developed by a New Zealand dairy farmer and
eagerly adopted by conscientious parents in Britain. Having been, I felt, a
victim of this tyranny, I wanted none of it, but on the other hand how nice
it would be to be rid of nappies, I thought, and let her give it a try, with
some success. A suitcase full of new clothes and toys came separately by rail,
which for us felt like Christmas all over again, and we had of course the
endless round of tea parties and the odd clinic visit – Mum found the sister
very stern and disagreeable. In Gwelo Paul had his first proper hair cut and
came out looking a real boy; at Bata Shoes we bought him his first red

Paul with his England Granny

leather shoes, fortunately made for wide feet more used to going unshod. After much foot waving and clomping about, the novelty wore off and he went back to barefoot, like most of the rest of the population. Once more we were invited to the Cummings' farm, where Mark and I glowed as our landlords told her what perfect tenants we had been.

Mark had managed to schedule some leave while she was with us, and we took Mum on a tour, going as far as the Eastern Highlands, where we had honeymooned, and which had, we felt, the most beautiful scenery in Southern Rhodesia. The Mini Traveller bucketed along, which can't have been comfortable for Mum, but she insisted on sitting in the back with Paul, and they also shared hotel bedrooms, Granny with potty at the ready. Our route took us first, via Selukwe and its pretty tree-clad hills, to Fort Victoria (now Masvingo), so that we could show Mum the nearby Great Zimbabwe Ruins.

This was a mysterious place, a huge site with the remains of high curved granite stone walls many feet thick. There was a Great Enclosure with a conical tower almost phallic in its effect; everywhere sinuous curves, with not a right angle in sight. The craftsmanship was superb: precisely cut stones

Our house in Abercorn: brother Will
with Paul on the embryo lawn

With the travellers: L to R Simon,
self, Mark with Paul, Will

Happy days:
Abercorn Yacht
Club on a typical
Sunday

Will (L) with Carl Kuhne,
Robin Crosse-Upcott and
Cessna – International Red
Locust Control Service

Rigging dinghies for a sail, Colin
Carlin (R) supervising
(Paul's minder Uelo out of shot!)

Westie's stores on
Marshall Avenue,
Abercorn's main street

Romance – and
oil supplies

Mpulungu: S.S. Liemba, sacks of dried fish and brother Simon (R)

Sisters Romana (L) and
Amabilis: a day off on the lake

Mark, his clerk and Paul
at Mpulungu depot

Hats and gloves for Caroline's
Christening: Caroline with her
godmother Jiff and me, plus
guests

Kalambo Falls: holding
Paul tight, with his
Cape Town granny

Lake Tanganyika
regatta picnic: self
proposing a toast
as Caroline
balances against
Dad's knee, centre
foreground

fitting securely without mortar in walls up to 11 metres high and six metres thick. It was a strange, moving place in the middle of nowhere – so how on earth was it created, we wondered, and by whom? The one thing we knew with certainty was that it could not have been built by local people: after all, they lived in mud huts – hadn't even invented the wheel! We accepted the alternative explanations that had been developed over decades – that the builders had been Arabs, or Phoenicians (though why they should have picked this place was still a mystery); there was even a legend that this was a replica of the palace of the Queen of Sheba in Jerusalem. All these exotic and improbable theories only added to the atmosphere of the place.

***

Cousin John's photo of young Yvonne shows Great Zimbabwe's magnificent stonework

Mark and Simon (on an earlier visit) pondering the mysteries of the Ruins

Even more fascinating for me has been learning, decades after our visit, the truth behind the legends – truth emerging from archaeological research through the 20th century. As far back as 1928 an English woman archaeologist, Gertrude Caton-Thompson, was first to state that the ruins were of decidedly African origin. Since then artefacts found, radiocarbon dating and more archaeological research have established that the structures, which extend over 1800 acres, were built over the 11th to 15th centuries, by a people who spoke one of the Shona languages and so were members of the Bantu family of African peoples. Over 300 stone structures have been found on the Great Zimbabwe site itself, from simple to more elaborate; pottery, coins and beads etc. found originated from as far away as China, the Middle East and India, suggesting that it was a great trading centre, with gold from mines in the area at the heart of its wealth.

Not that it was easy for white people to accept these facts. In colonial Rhodesia the ruins' true origins were hushed up, Ian Smith's government pressurising the Museum Service to withhold the correct information. The Inspector of Monuments, Peter Garlake, whose research had been first to prove incontrovertibly that it had been constructed by ancestors of the current local population, and who refused to toe the government line, was forced out. Another Museum service official, Paul Sinclair, quoted in '*None but Ourselves*' by Julie Frederikse (1990) said : *Once a member of the Museum Board of Trustees threatened me with losing my job if I said publicly that blacks had built Zimbabwe*'.

Great Zimbabwe Ruins became a UNESCO World Heritage Site in 1986.

***

As we headed up into the Eastern Highlands, Mum's new hobby came to the fore. On the rutted dirt roads, with panoramic views before us, she would suddenly call to Mark, regardless of dangerous bends, 'Oh do stop, please!' She had spotted what looked like another interesting wild flower. These she would pick – if there was more than one – and at our next hotel would sketch them in her notebook. At one of our highest points, we stopped to admire the view next to an abandoned steamroller, where Paul

Eastern Highlands: Paul's first Top Gear moment

Mountain Lodge, Vumba – return of the honeymooners

had his first 'Top Gear moment'. Installed by Dad in the driving seat, he sat turning and turning the disengaged steering wheel until we had to tear him away, protesting bitterly. It was a very happy time for all of us, out of our normal routine, enjoying each other's company, all of us centred around Paul.

Back in Gwelo, Mum made a planned trip to Bulawayo to stay with our Watson cousins, and to connect with her beloved Mothers' Union. When we were growing up, we had experienced the 'MU' as a nuisance, diverting our mother's attention from us; only much later did I learn of its valuable work overseas, its network spreading deep into the African continent, and into townships where white people seldom went. Needless to say, Mum had organised to join what I referred to in my 'welcome to Africa letter' as a 'jamboree' in an African township outside Bulawayo. She described on her return a great hangar of a church, a vast gathering of ladies dressed in white with splendid head-dresses, and how the service came alive with hymns sung in a vibrant close harmony that seemed miraculously spontaneous and effortless.

After the now usual goodbye parties in Gwelo, suddenly Mum was gone, flying back from Salisbury to Britain and their new home, the old vicarage she and Pa were restoring on the Herts/Cambs border. She took with her a copy of the Rhodesia Herald ('established 1891') for 23 April 1963, filed it away with my letters. Its yellowed broadsheet pages bring me a feel of that Salisbury, of those times, like a scent captured in a bottle. It was St George's Day, 50th anniversary of the laying of the Cathedral's foundation stone. The Southern Rhodesia government was declaring war on juvenile delinquents; the city was 'shivering through one of its coldest April days ever' (62.4 F at midday). In London, the United Nations Sub-committee on Colonialism had been told 'politely but firmly that the British government cannot permit any interference in the domestic affairs of Southern Rhodesia'. On an inside page, the editor had seized gleefully on a piece from the Yorkshire Post, thundering that 'an Eskimo would be as well qualified to advise on how to fight bush fires as the U.N. Sub-Committee on Colonialism is to advise Britain on political affairs'. The new Prime Minister, Mr Winston Field [shortly to be succeeded by Ian Smith] had written to Mr Rab Butler, First Secretary of State, repeating that Southern Rhodesia 'must be given independence on the day that either Northern Rhodesia or Nyasaland secedes or gains independence'. Beside an advertisement for French velvets at 29s 6d a yard, the U.S. 7th Fleet was reported to be sailing into the Gulf of Siam amidst concern over developments in Laos, while President Kennedy was meeting with his National Security Council. Further on, amidst advertisements for Windolene and Brisk soap, an African had been sentenced to death for murder in Ndola, tourist numbers were down 5% 'due to news reports'. Joshua Nkomo (who had recently testified to the UN Sub-Committee on Colonialism, urging them to intervene in Southern Rhodesia) was expected to appeal against his conviction and sentence to six months hard labour for 'assaulting, resisting or obstructing police officers'. Meanwhile in Lusaka, Mr Martin Kaunda, a well-known teacher, had been accepted as 'the first African south of Uganda to join the Rotary Club'. Helen Shapiro, 'Britain's raven-haired 16-year old singing sensation' would soon be appearing at the Palace. On the tobacco auction floor, sales for the previous day were 2,068,535 lbs, at an average price per pound of 37.16 pence. Trading in copper from Northern Rhodesia's mines was slow.

Both Paul and I felt doleful at Mum's departure, Paul was whiney and clingy at the loss of so much loving and undivided attention, I with a sudden sense that little stood now between us and our transfer to the back of beyond. Was Mark anxious too at this big career leap, and a posting so far from branch office support? I think we would have both been too busy making the best of it to bring our anxieties into the open. My own were eased a little by a visit from Paul Scotcher who, after a couple of years as the Abercorn rep, would soon be handing over to Mark. They spent some time talking work over their beers, and when I joined them he described life there: a great place, he said, good social club, sailing, families with young kids – you'll soon make friends. But, he added, shopping is a bit of a problem, you have to order a lot – and take every stick of furniture you need. This meant shopping, which was anathema to us for the strains it put on our budget.

By late May I suspected I was pregnant, thrilled to have it confirmed before we left Gwelo. I had explained to Mark my longing to have children closer together in age than I was to my own three brothers. The oldest, Will, was 3½ years younger than me and I wanted my children to have a better chance of growing up in a closer relationship and enjoying each others' company. Now busy with endless decisions of what to take and what to throw, hauling out our battered suitcases for packing, I was not so thrilled at the inconvenient morning sickness that suddenly beset me. I was going to lose my support system too, those more experienced mums who had seen me through the first pregnancy and Paul's birth. We sadly did the rounds of farewell parties with couples who had become good friends, swearing to correspond, to keep up with each others' family news. Whilst I am sure we all meant it, at the same time I somehow sensed we were unlikely ever to see each other again.

Our little Mini was to take us as far as the Copper Belt, but with no room for Boy. We organised for Mark's colleague Doug to have him flown up once we arrived, while Twist the cat found a new home with the Arkwrights. Daniel meanwhile had decided to return to Nyasaland. It had never occurred to us to suggest he and Inez come with us, it was far too remote for that. As I had sorted and packed, a small heap of unwanted clothes had grown until they filled a big old cardboard suitcase. Now, with the house echoing and empty, cleaned for the last time by Daniel, we all stood at the back door, dressed in our travelling clothes, the back of the Mini piled high. We presented Daniel with the battered case, and Mark handed him his savings account pass book, into which we had deposited a small amount each month, with strict instructions to use it wisely. Daniel took it with cupped hands and a respectful 'Yes baas, thank you baas,' in his soft voice. I looked at Inez: was her waist filling out, or was I imagining it? I did not like to ask. They climbed into Mark's Zephyr for a lift to the station, while Paul and I waited for the Cummings to come and take the keys from us.

Daniel: A Postscript

A couple of weeks after we arrived in Northern Rhodesia, a letter arrived for Mark from the BSA (Southern Rhodesian) Police. It reported that a native, Daniel xxx, had been found to have in his possession a suitcase of clothes that clearly belonged to a European. The native claimed that these had been given to him. Would the addressee now please confirm if this claim was correct, so that the native could be released, otherwise the matter would have to be further investigated.

We were furious: honest Daniel, now held at the border on account of an old suitcase of cast-offs! Too late we realised that we should have foreseen this and issued a letter to him in the first place. Mark hastily wrote a stiff note confirming the gift and we just hoped that it would get there.

Long Distance

All morning I've been reading my old letters home,
the crumpled aerogrammes and flimsy sheets
rustling from airmail envelopes.

Here in the margin, 15 December 1961,
I'd written our phone number – had added
'a party line I fear, so we'll ring you'.

Gwelo 362327: studying the digits, I'm seized
with longing to reach for the phone: to check
the country's codes, punch in the numbers,

wait for the connecting hums and clicks, to hear
the faint ring-ring … ring-ring … and then at last
my own young voice, bright with energy: 'Hello?'

PART II

Northern Rhodesia

CHAPTER 8

Abercorn – a very particular place

Sometimes, still, I will meet someone who was 'out in Africa' – Rhodesia, they might say, perhaps Northern Rhodesia for a while. Place names are exchanged and – surprisingly often considering its size – Abercorn is mentioned. 'I lived there', I will say, and we'll smile at each other: 'Ah yes, Abercorn …' For it was indeed a very particular place.

I say 'was' not only because it is called Mbala now, having reverted after independence to its pre-colonial name, but because the Abercorn I knew and the life I led there as a very young woman revolved around a community of some 200 white people, a colonial settlement that was, we found, already changing. But I am getting ahead of myself. In June 1963 the little weekly Dakota delivered Paul and me to Abercorn's airfield through bumpy turbulence and into a rainstorm. How mightily relieved I had been to escape the Copper Belt where we had spent a fortnight best forgotten: while Mark was in the office on his induction, I had attempted to manage with Paul and nothing to do in the hotel from hell. It was a struggle to get the kitchens to produce anything suitable for a toddler's meals, let alone when he needed them; there was no safe place for him to play or run around and oddly, no hospitality forthcoming from local company wives. And I was suffering from morning sickness, this time much worse than with my first pregnancy.

There was therefore something deeply comforting about being met off the plane by a friendly face – Audrey Scotcher, wife of Mark's predecessor, with two of her six children in tow. 'We'll go to the hotel later,' she said, 'first we're out to tea'. From her car I glimpsed a main street of sorts, with a couple of general stores, some kind of municipal office building, then bungalows, widely spaced along dirt roads, with flat-topped spindly African trees – 'miombo' I later learned – through which shone little Lake Chila, Audrey pointing out the Yacht Club's boat house on the opposite bank.

So, over cups of tea, the second person I met was Jennifer Bowmaker, whose husband, Alan, was a provincial fisheries officer, their little Jeanne a year younger than Paul. Children and their toys at our feet, we discovered we had good friends in Cape Town in common; somehow that anchored me, gave me a sense of being in a place not so strange after all, however far it might be from 'civilisation'.

We were to rent a house, but the Scotchers', although overlooking Lake Chila, was too large and expensive for us and we were advised that other possibilities were coming up. Meanwhile the Lake View Hotel outside town fulfilled its name, the view this time being over Lake Tanganyika some twenty miles and two thousand feet below. And beyond, in the far distance, I could see for the first time the misty blue bulk of high mountains behind which, I knew, lay the Congo. I thought of it with a sort of dread, for all its violence, coup and counter-coup continued to be regularly reported in the papers, with the exploits of mercenary forces, the seemingly endless slaughter and bloodshed. The hotel though was restorative, being everything the previous one had not been: *so easy with Paul, gardens all round, no road worry, large verandah, meals easily got and a nice manageress ... the car won't be here for a week* [it was being transported by road] *but I don't need one till we settle a house ... The planes come in Weds/ Thurs, NB for posting ex U.K Sun/Mon.* My mother underlined this last bit of that first letter from Northern Rhodesia, for it was to dictate a schedule which was to become an important feature in our respective weekly routines.

Abercorn was where we were to live, but much of the focus of Mark's job as an oil company rep. was elsewhere. Firstly he had a huge geographical area to cover, albeit sparsely settled, on very rough dirt roads, dusty in the dry season, often all but impassable in the rains. And then there was the company depot down at Mpulungu, a small fishing port on Lake Tanganyika. Every alternate Sunday the S.S. Liemba steamed down the lake from Kigoma in Tanganyika, towing a petroleum products laden barge, to be discharged into the company's storage tanks. This routine, together with the size of his 'patch', was to make substantial demands on Mark and on our life together.

Over those first weeks we began to get our bearings. Abercorn stood – Mbala still stands – on the escarpment above Lake Tanganyika at the end of the western Great Rift Valley. It was Northern Rhodesia's most northerly town, and on early maps of Southern Africa in the 1890's there it is, marking the British Empire's stake in the region. Now however it lay at the end of the Great North Road, most of which was unmetalled, and as we had been warned, was also some 400 miles from the nearest railhead, with all the implications for access to supplies. It is also the country's highest town, some 5,400 feet (1670 m) above sea level, which meant that despite being so much closer to the Equator than where we had been living, the climate was pleasant, avoiding the extreme heat that met you as you descended to Mpulungu. Among its 200 or so white residents – the 'Europeans' – were the settlers on their outlying farms, civil servants with the Northern Rhodesia Government, others working for related organisations. There was a town management board for a township area that included around 3,500 Africans of the Bemba tribe, these latter still mainly living at that time in Mbulu township a short distance from the 'centre'. Two hospitals were run by nuns of a Roman Catholic order, the Sisters of the Sacred Hearts of Jesus and Mary, one in the township, the other a bungalow near Lake Chila opened only for the occasional white patient. Abercorn was headquarters of the International Red Locust Control Service (IRLCS), its planes and later helicopters monitoring and spraying the marshlands of Northern Rhodesia's Mweru swamp and the Rukwa Valley in southern Tanzania. The organisation was shrinking now and its staff houses becoming available to rent.

The political situation was very different from our previous postings too. I should admit here that it was only recently that I fully understood the difference between a colony (for example Southern Rhodesia) and a protectorate, which was Northern Rhodesia's current status. Whilst the former had always been left pretty much to its own devices, with a British-appointed Governor General, the latter was run by an administrative service recruited, trained and employed by the Colonial Office in London. Its people worked even in the remotest corners of the country, administering everything from justice to health to infrastructure development, and working closely with local chiefs. All this is vividly described in Ian Mackinson's autobiography *Footprints in the Dust* in his account of his years as one of those administrators. As I now recognise, it was a world away from my own English-speaking, small town based experience of life in the country.

***

Although Northern Rhodesia shared half its name with its southern neighbour, it was a very different country, '*a vast, scarcely developed, hardly populated area with a tiny metal spine*' as Doris Lessing described it in her 1957 memoir *Going Home,* the 'metal spine' being the towns of its Copper Belt where two great mining companies extracted and exported its vast mineral wealth. South of the Copper Belt was the country's capital, Lusaka. The European population was concentrated in these urban areas which, to the Africans, were places to find work, from which they returned to their rural homes.

The country's nationalist movement had always opposed the idea of Federation, seeing it as a way for its southern neighbour, so close to South

Africa and with its much larger white population, to take advantage of their country's mineral wealth and to draw it closer to a quasi-apartheid system and legislation they so detested. Northern Rhodesia's Africans wanted to keep their land, not be constrained within overcrowded Native Reserves. They wanted the independence their northern neighbours had already achieved.

With Harold Macmillan's Wind of Change speech during his visit to the African colonies in 1960/61, with the rapid gaining of independence of all France's colonies south of the Sahara, with Britain's West and East Africa colonies gaining theirs too, break-up of the Federation became inevitable. In October 1962 the final version of Northern Rhodesia's new constitution produced an African majority on its Legislative Council, as neighbouring Nyasaland's had. By the end of that year (just as we were to learn of our impending move from Gwelo to Abercorn) all support for the Federation was at an end. Nyasaland, under its nationalist leader Dr. Hastings Banda, back from England where he had practised as a G.P., was to secede. In March 1963, after continued wrangling between the parties, and the Southern Rhodesian elections that had brought in the Rhodesia Front, the British Government decided that Northern Rhodesia too must be allowed to secede. Independence was in sight at last and the Central African Federation would, by the end of 1963, be no more. Final elections to the legislative council in the coming January 1964 would lead to self-government.

***

At last we found a suitable house that we could afford – which meant that it was time to engage a servant and to get used to shopping in this new environment. In such a rural area, there was not a great pool of trained servants to choose from; I think we took on someone recommended by one of the families leaving as we arrived. So we took on Daudi, a tall, silent man with what I read as a slightly disdainful expression, which made me feel very uncomfortable. His first task was to rid all our furniture of the layers of dust that it had accumulated on its journey along hundreds of miles of dirt roads. I had established to my relief that he could bake bread. I had been very anxious about this, needlessly as it turned out, discovering that it was one of the routine skills servants learned for Abercorn's white households (the District Commissioner's cook, I recall, had been trained at a bakery and could whip up all sorts of breads from cottage loaves to plaits and poppy seed rolls).

Shopping needed a different routine from Gwelo. There were three general stores on the main street, Marshall Avenue, though as we had been warned they carried a limited range largely for the local African market. Our main port of call was Westwoods Stores – known to all as Westies – with its butchery next door for cheaper cuts and servants' ration meat, nothing fancy. However, if you wanted dairy products, or particular cuts of meat, you had to order them from Ndola, whence they were delivered once a fortnight in a refrigerated truck. Never having been a great planner, this took some getting used to, particularly as so much of the entertaining we did was at short notice, for if any company men were in the area, we would inevitably invite them round for a meal. I recall depending a great deal on tins, including ghee for butter and evaporated milk for cream in emergencies. I was longing to be installed in our permanent home and start up a vegetable garden too.

At last we were able to move in. It was another iron-roofed bungalow, this time with a wide entrance set back between its two front rooms, forming a sort of terrace. Oddly, there was no stoep. It was the last house on a small dirt road that meandered off into the bush, heading to nowhere we needed to go. I tried hard to become accustomed to Daudi, but wrote home ominously '*I don't care for him, he's not a patch on Daniel but there's no choice up here.*' I think now that, while Daniel was undoubtedly more skilled and with an easier temperament, the size of our Abercorn house did not help. In Gwelo we had had large rooms and an extensive garden too, with Daniel deployed in both. Here we had a much smaller bungalow and I felt oppressed by this constant looming presence, silently resistant to my attempts to get him to do things my way. Fortunately both Paul and I liked Uelo, our young and cheerful garden boy, who didn't mind being told how to work, and who played happily with Paul while I was at my sewing machine, initially altering curtains for our smaller rooms.

We had hardly settled in when we had news of our next house guests. My eldest brother Will was just coming down from Oxford and had some months to kill before writing exams for the Civil Service. He and Simon, now also at Oxford and with the long summer vac. before him, had hatched a plot to travel overland and visit us. 'It's not that far, is it?' they said to each other over an atlas in the college library. Only around 6,000 miles, via Marseilles, Alexandria, Cairo, Khartoum, Nairobi and across Tanganyika to the border with Northern Rhodesia. The single communication we received from them en route was from Cairo, where they were trying to get visas for Sudan, and where Will learned of his law degree from a back number of the Times in the British Council's reading room. We could only hope they would turn up some time. I got busy with fresh curtains for the guest room.

Out of the blue I was approached by Dave Millar, who with his wife Dido ran the little primary school for white children, and who was to direct the next amateur dramatics production. This was an American comedy and suddenly they were short of a leading lady – would I please, please audition for the part? It didn't matter, apparently, that my last appearance on a stage had been as an extra in a school production of Gilbert and Sullivan's Pirates of Penzance; they would coach me, show me the ropes and I would have a very experienced leading man for my husband!

It sounds fun, I thought. Flattered, curious and unable to resist the challenge, I agreed to audition – was immediately offered the part and, ignoring my pregnancy and the obvious heavy commitments on my time, accepted. The play was *The Gazebo* and had been on in London's West End a few years before, then made into a film. The plot swirled with deception, intrigue, blackmail and mistaken identity, yet was amusing and light and of course all ended happily. I was to play Nell, television actress and loving wife of successful playwright Elliott, living on Long Island. His was the biggest part, played by an experienced amdram actor, an older man who worked in local government. The third large part, of the couple's neighbour, a district attorney, was taken by Chris Roberts, the medical officer, and there were a number of smaller character parts. I was on stage a good deal of the time and had seven costume changes over the three acts.

I was immediately swept into the hard work of line-learning and a routine of endless rehearsals over four weeks, while Mark, when he was not away, helped to construct the set. We started with dialogue, moved on to movement and gestures and dovetailing our parts. I was fortunate in having my leading man – we'll call him Roy – to show me the ropes. Fortunate, that is, until, thrown together in frequent rehearsals as an affectionate couple, he suddenly decided that he had fallen in love with me. Roy himself did not really attract me, I think I was mainly seduced by the flattery of being so desired by an older, married man (in his late 30's I would guess). Nothing happened between us other than a few clandestine, relatively chaste meetings and, naïve and simplistic as I was, I was sure that the whole thing would die down without anyone knowing about it. Perhaps it would have, had it not been for his wife discovering that Roy's attentions were elsewhere. She demanded he pull out and end it (which would also have meant the end of the production). When he refused she took their several children and departed to the bush camp down at Mpulungu, whereupon the news was around the community in a trice. Someone broke it to Mark as he returned from a business trip; he, poor man, was devastated, whilst I, faced with the reality of what I had allowed to happen, was horrified and embarrassed. My defensive wail of 'but we haven't *done* anything!' was of course only of limited comfort to him. Deep down I felt very bad about it, both for him and for our relationship, but also for myself, wondering what people would think of me, in such a small community where I was as yet hardly known. Mark was also under great pressure from his new job, which did not help either of us. Somehow we patched things up, managing to have some quiet weekend time together with golf, bridge with our new neighbours the Crosse-Upcotts, and Sunday sailing. However, Mark must continue to travel, spending nights away from home, and I to rehearse, practising my portrayal of a successful actress and affectionate wife whilst in private fending off Roy's pleas for time alone together. Of course none of this reached my letters home, merely: *It still seems to need hours more rehearsal but I suppose it will work out. Bookings are going well anyway. Today I must gather my wardrobe of seven outfits together! I was getting rather tired,* [by now I was 3 ½ months pregnant] *with late rehearsals and too much other activity as well, so I am now taking things easier during the day (no golf etc.) and feel a lot better.*

On the Tuesday before the big night, while Mark was away in Kasama, I received a telegram from Will and Simon: they planned to be at Tunduma, about 100 miles away on the Tanganyika/Northern Rhodesia border, by sundown on Thursday. Could Mark meet them? I phoned him in Kasama and he decided that he could fit this detour into his schedule, though we were by no means certain that they would make it, for they were dependent on lifts along a little used bush road for this last stage. Nonetheless, in mid-dress rehearsal on Thursday, someone whispered to me that they had arrived, and there at the back of the hall I could make out the three shadowy figures. It was all I could do not to leap off the stage and run to greet them.

My goodness, but they were thin! They had had a very tough time and had spent much of their four weeks on survival rations, as their travellers' tales soon revealed. As Will summarises it now: *We had spent about six weeks, one hundred pounds, on four different boats over 15 days, five days on four different trains, arranged lifts in cars for 1500 miles over three days (the lengths of France and later of Tanzania), hitchhiking too many cars and lorries to count, and now we had made it!*

On the day of the performance, a totally unexpected and tragic event nearly caused it to be cancelled. A farmer, John Macrae, from a prominent and popular local family, had returned from a bush trip seriously ill, and had been diagnosed with acute poliomyelitis. The government surgeon flew up by special plane and he and Chris Roberts would have flown John down to hospital on the Copper Belt, had he not been too ill to move. Chris gallantly stuck with his part in the play, and it went ahead, although everyone in the cast was very conscious of the anxiety and dismay among the audience. After all those rehearsals, I suddenly felt daunted as I peeped through the curtains at the packed hall, but once the house lights lowered, shadowy faces looking up at the stage, the adrenaline kicked in and I was into the swing of it. I loved every minute of it, secretly revelling in all that attention, even managing my many changes without mishap. After our curtain calls, Chris reverted to his medical officer role and stepped forward to advise us all to take strict hygiene precautions, but that as polio vaccine would take six weeks to be effective, there was no purpose in urgent immunisation. Fortunately Mark, Paul and I had all had the sugar lump in Gwelo. There was a post-show party at someone's house and we were very late to bed, while Chris sat up with John. He was subsequently flown to Ndola and an iron lung, where tragically he died, leaving a wife and very young family.

(There was, however, much speculation about the real cause of John's death, and rumours swirled in the community. John had grown up in the area, knew it and its people well and spoke chi-Bemba fluently. It was said that, in one of his bush trips, he had in some way offended the spirits of a place sacred to the tribe – was this why he was struck down with the illness that would kill him? Vengeful spirits? An angry Chief? 'All the locals knew this was why he died,' Jiff Bowmaker now reminds me, 'and – well, you can't just discount these things, can you?')

Abercorn had its own little monthly newspaper, quirkily named *Abercornucopia*. It was produced and largely written by John Carlin, a retired journalist who ran the Lake Press in the town, its main business coming from government printing contracts. The following week, a write-up of the play appeared, with the headline *NEW STAR IN BRILLIANT SHOW.* I had reason to be grateful to John for his piece, not just because it was flattering about my performance, describing me as: *an excellent actress – well among the very best ever seen in Abercorn* but in particular for this: *The part was that of a successful young actress – and a successful young actress she was. She was also the beloved wife of a television writer – and his beloved wife she duly was. She made the whole thing natural and credible...* Still smarting under the embarrassment of being seen as the cause of a very public marital crisis, I felt that he had understood – that I had been, after all, only acting the part that I was required to play. I do not recall having any more contact with Roy after that night, and it was not long before he was posted elsewhere. There were to be a number of other productions during our time in Abercorn, at least one of which sparked a domestic upset far more dramatic than ours. I remember particularly being asked to be in Noel Coward's *Hay Fever,* to play the part of Amanda, indeed. I wrote home that I had no time and that anyway 'I don't care for the play'.

The minute my brothers arrived, I started cooking to try to satisfy their travel-induced hunger, and for the next few weeks was producing three cooked meals a day. Soon I had to write home and ask Mum to supplement our budget, to keep up with their appetites. However much I brought to table, down it went, until that is my economy dish 'bacon and potato bake' resulted in a traumatic incident. Over lunch Will suddenly choked – a hard-baked slice of potato topping had got wedged in his throat. We tried everything: whacking him on the back, glasses of water, finally had to resort to calling Chris Roberts. Hours later, now in the little 'European' hospital, with Will more and more exhausted and in pain, Chris was talking of having to fly him down to Kasama, where there was a larger, better equipped hospital. And then suddenly, the potato slice shifted, softened perhaps over time, and he was back home, shaky but recovering. I never cooked that economy dish again.

With the hard work of the play over, we could spend time showing Will and Simon Abercorn and the area, exploring it ourselves as we did so. There was the daily routine, of course, becoming familiar to us but strange and interesting for them: the local, limited shopping at Westie's Stores and the Indian run general store. Nearby on the main street was a small lending library at the Victoria Memorial Institute which, though strong on Africana, left me thankful for the parcels of Penguins my father sent. And if it was Wednesday or Thursday, then there were probably letters from home on the arriving plane, and of course our own aerogrammes home to be timed to 'catch the post'. (This was a long-standing family catch phrase, from my mother's passion for letter writing and for making a dash down the hill to the local stores to catch the 4.30 collection.)

We organised for Will and Simon to visit the headquarters of International Red Locust Control Service (IRLCS) to meet the pilots and get an offer of a flight, flying low over the herds of game that roamed the area. Flying very low (down to 20 feet) though risky, was necessary, for the grounded locusts must first be flushed out and, once in flight, sprayed. Ian Mackinson in his memoir tells of an occasion when, flying with Robin Crosse-Upcott, the wheels of the Cessna just touched an elephant's back, and 'with a considerable lurch and superb control by Robin' the plane was righted, later landing safely back in Abercorn. Mark went up once with Robin too, a neighbour of ours; ex-RAF, he looked like a pilot from a war film with his upright demeanour and classic features, distinguished grey hair and black moustache. He had spotted an albino giraffe and sold photographs of it to National Geographic magazine, and they went in search of it again. I still have the tiny black and white print Mark took of it from the plane's window.

We took my brothers down the rough dirt road to Lake Tanganyika, twisting through wooded slopes, always descending. We were greeted at the oil depot on the lake shore by humid heat and a pungent smell of 'dagaa' – tiny sardine-like fish dried in the sun, packed into huge sacks and despatched inland. At night fishermen would go out, their lights shining down onto the deep waters to attract the silver shoals into their nets. Up in Abercorn you could buy their larger catch, a type of nile perch, fresh – well, fairly fresh and big enough to slice into steaks of firm white flesh, a change from endless meat, if not very fine flavoured. We watched the 'S.S. Liemba' steam down the lake one Sunday afternoon, looking for all the world like the German boat spotted by Katharine Hepburn and Humphrey Bogart in 'The African Queen'. Which was not surprising, for the vessel had started life as the 'Graf von Götzen', used by the Germans, based in what was then German East Africa (subsequently Tanganyika) to control the lake in World War I. When, in 1916, the German commander abandoned the port of Kigoma to head south, he scuttled his prize vessel. But it was later resurrected and renamed the 'S.S. Liemba' (Liemba was the name of the lake when Dr Livingstone 'discovered' it). The Germans' defeat is vividly and hilariously described by Giles Foden in 'Mimi and Toutou Go Forth – the bizarre battle of Lake Tanganyika'. The film 'The African Queen' had indeed been made in the area, the film crew based in the then Belgian Congo just up the western shore, though sadly the steam ship they used was not the Liemba, but another, on Lake Victoria. More recently Michael Palin in the television series 'Pole to Pole' spent an uncomfortable night on the Liemba, as he made his way south towards Cape Town.

Lake Tanganyika is remarkable: the third largest freshwater lake in the world, the second deepest after Lake Baikal, nearly 5,000 feet at its deepest. At over 400 miles long and averaging 31 miles wide, it is the largest rift lake in Africa, and the great depth of its tropical waters means that much of its lower depths are 'dead' or 'fossil water' and its extensive fish life is found only in the topmost 600 feet of water. It is fed by three rivers including the Kalambo not far from Mpulungu, and its waters flow out into the Congo River system and eventually into the Atlantic Ocean. I did not have all those figures in my head at the time: all I knew was that it was immensely deep, that its size meant that being on open water could feel like being at sea and that, situated as it was between two towering mountain ranges, storms and high winds could whip up unexpectedly.

After the lake, we visited the other local attraction, the Kalambo Falls, second highest waterfall in Africa. I remember how tightly I clung to Paul, for there was no sightseeing platform here – just a stony track and the sudden falling away of the earth before us, the distant thunder of the water below. Even in the dry season it was an impressive sight, the waters creaming away in one uninterrupted drop of over 700 feet, from the high east African plateau over the shelf of the Great Rift Valley. There were long views over distant Lake Tanganyika, with beyond it the huge blue-misty bulk of Northern Rhodesia's western mountain ranges; rare maribou storks, strangely angular birds, floated on the thermals in front of the spray.

Having made my brothers temporary members of the Abercorn Club, they could join us in tennis, learning to sail and socialising in the club house. It was a happy time for all of us, for me a precious connection with home and my parents, hearing of their new home and its on-going restoration. Paul was developing fast, and at his Granny's prodding I reported, along with accounts of our doings, his progress on the pot, with feeding himself and lists of his first words. He adored his two young uncles who were always ready to play, or to allow him to 'help' them in the garden. The three of us had been brought up knowing that gardening was something you did, once you had a home of your own, so it was not hard to harness their labour, though I seem to have made no concessions to the fact that we were now into the hottest, driest time of the year: *The garden is slowly being transformed*, I wrote, *Will has built a rich compost heap, I have had 2 flower beds right out and put back again enriched and replanted, and now Uelo is hacking at new beds round where lawn will be started when the rains come. V. hard work as it's so dry (Simon can testify!). Lots of seeds coming up incl. dahlias and carnations. We have some crazy paving to do but shrink from the labour.* No wonder our visitors needed all that food! Paul would follow the workers around with his pull-along truck, or a small watering can. In the evenings Mark and I taught Will and Simon bridge to make an in-house foursome, which apparently we all much enjoyed – a very odd thought to me now, having not played it since.

Despite my expanding waistline I felt very fit *'and obviously the tiny does too, as it is fantastically active for five months, leaping around'* I wrote. So I could continue, for the time being, to learn to sail, crewing for experienced skippers like Alan and Colin Carlin. Playing golf under Mark's coaching was still a source of togetherness for the two of us, with Paul pushed in his pushchair by Uelo and just about tolerating nine holes if rewarded with chips of spicy dried game biltong. In the club house afterwards, sitting in state on the bar, he would be given sips of beer from our glasses. Down at the Yacht Club, dinghy racing was for Sundays, so during the week we would take a couple of the smaller boats and sail them to a little beach on some other part of the shore for a picnic. The Yacht Club, I wrote, was now Paul's second home.

Abruptly, after our weeks of fun together, Will and Simon were gone: Simon flying home to the new year at Oxford, Will, who still had a few months free, for some sightseeing and temporary work in Lusaka. Once more the end of a happy family visit left us all feeling bereft.

Slide Show

Colour transparencies slide from the envelope.
Soon they'll be reborn as jpeg files
that spring to life on my computer screen.
For now, I hold each one up to the light
like looking wrong way down a telescope.

I squint at tiny distant images:
a squatting toddler in a stripy T shirt
points at a line of hairy caterpillars;
a youth and a young woman, all tanned legs
and bright bleached hair, raise a dinghy's sail;
late sun on silhouetted laughing faces,
an open picnic case, calm distant water.

And here's a couple, back to camera, each
following the tyre track of a red-dirt road,
she with a push chair, a high ridge of grass
running between them. On the slide's frame
someone's scribble in long faded ink:
The happy pair stride into Africa.

CHAPTER 9

'Its pride is its people' – but shopping is a challenge

By now it had become clear to me how much could not be bought locally, and an abiding theme of my letters from Abercorn was how to obtain the unobtainable. Some things could be sent for from the Copper Belt, or fetched by anyone driving down who had the space available. On Mark's occasional trips to Ndola he would be charged with bringing back assorted household and garden items from plastic pants to garden fertiliser. With October upon us, Christmas was already an endless preoccupation, with cards to be ordered through Mum, airmailed to us, written and, in the case of those destined for UK addresses, returned to her for posting. I worried at what gifts to send family, when there was so little available, and sent for catalogues from the Army and Navy Stores in London. I wonder now why my parents didn't just say 'Look, don't worry to send anything, we realise it is all too difficult.' Perhaps they did, and I was insisting on keeping our end up.

As for clothes, I was now even more thankful for my sewing machine and the dressmaking evening course I had done in London, for fabrics were one thing we could buy locally from an Indian run store: *All alone Paul and I are now, as Mark is away for 3 days,* I wrote after my brothers' departure, *it seems very odd, but fortunately I have so much to do that I don't have time to sit and be sad… Paul misses his uncles very much, but is being pretty good considering all. I am in the middle of making him 2 shirts, 2 prs shorts and some pyjamas, not to mention a dress for Shirley Macd's new daughter and a smock for me.* After my pregnancy, and as the pace of our social life hotted up, my letters would refer to yet another party dress I was running up a couple of days before the event. I remember with particular affection an off-one-shoulder number I made in a white silky knit that draped in an elegant Grecian way. Making your own clothes, you can at least be sure that they fit well, we wives said to each other.

Then there were the really hard-to-find items, shoes being a particular problem, and here, as so often, I turned to Mum. Her workload in shopping and sending us parcels must have more than doubled once we were in Abercorn. Soon Mark's foot was traced so that a pair of Hush Puppies advertised in Punch could be bought and sent from England. And in late March of the following year would begin the Court Shoe Saga: *First, the enclosed cheque and cutting Ma: I saw this ad. for shoes which I think look v. nice, and I was hoping you cd. get me this very pair – 69/11. I am usually size 75B American so will have to risk the fit, and someone else would always buy them off me. It is impossible to get shoes from here and I am short of any decent ones. Colour I'd like would be anything from cream through to mushroom, wh. latter I'd like best.* In May, while Jiff's mother was visiting to help with the new baby, I enlisted her help when she returned to Salisbury, but in June I was enquiring : '*Did you eventually send any Joyce shoes (75B), I said no to Jiff's mother's offer from Salisbury as they were 89/11 there, and I might find some when I go down to the Copper Belt'.* I didn't, but would not give up, next turning to Mother in Cape Town, but drew a blank there too. Eventually, in late August: '*I am delighted to say the shoes arrived, and are perfect, couldn't be better if I'd tried them on first – I'm sure you're relieved all your efforts were worthwhile!*' It had taken five months, but I had my court shoes.

It serves to remind me of the sheer hard work my mother must have put in, trying to be a mum and granny at such a distance. Her poor parcel wrapping technique had been a standing family joke since boarding school, when crumpled bundles only just held together with ratty string lay on the hall table among other girls' neat offerings from home. Yet here she was still plugging away at the hated task: there were soon to be a Christmas cake in its Tupperware, then clothes for a new baby along with toys for Paul so he would not feel left out, ever more paperbacks for me, chosen by Pa. In one PS I managed a quick critique of William Faulkner's *As I Lay Dying* ('v. much enjoyed') and *The Sound and the Fury* ('terrific also I thought'). I wrote of one of her later cakes, for which she had delegated the wrapping: *'as I seized it off the P.O. counter all the string fell off around it – just in time! A note on it from Simon says "I wrapt this – Will tied it!"'*

Health care was another issue; no dentist locally, nor facilities for blood tests or other investigations. My blood group is negative, and this was going to require monitoring nearer my delivery date, for fear of a conflict with the baby's, Dr. Chris Roberts said, (he had informed me, 'against my wishes' that I was due around 21 January). The company general manager, up for a rare visit, assured us over dinner at the local hotel that the company would pay for my necessary trips to the Copper Belt, although in practice these turned out to be the subject of drawn out negotiations. Mark and I had already started to plan a combined shopping and health care trip for me.

Another emerging feature of Abercorn life was that residents – white residents – were leaving on an increasingly regular basis, often heading 'back to the U.K.' or 'down south', for now in late 1963 Northern Rhodesia was changing. Superficially many aspects of life in Abercorn continued as they had for decades: the club continued to thrive, although it seems amazing now that it did not yet admit black members; business continued to be done, the administration of the town and the province went on. But there were already signs of the end of Federation and of approaching independence. I began to write of parcel post slowing and my letters bore a new, Northern Rhodesia stamp. *Abercornucopia* surveyed the changing scene with a wary and often critical eye, and farewell parties at the club were more and more frequent. However, it was still a splendid place to live. Here is an extract from an extended feature on (largely white) Abercorn life, written by Tony Howard the following year for *Horizon*, the house magazine of a Copper Belt mining company. It was entitled '*The Town with a Twinkle in its Eye*':

Abercorn has self-assurance, without pomposity or priggishness, but rooted in the sure knowledge that it is a very superior place. It is not just that it has one of the most beautiful settings in Central Africa with hills behind and attractive little Lake Chila in front; nor is it that the town has the distinction of being the most northerly in the country; nor that at 5,400 ft. it stands on higher ground than any other town in Zambia; nor that its climate is such that people need never go away for their health's sake.

Abercorn's real pride is its people. The town has always attracted the kind of people who are out of the ruck, individualists. Many of the European population are civil servants who live there because their work dictates it, but Abercorn remains a place where most people live from choice.

One of Abercorn's most memorable features at that time was indeed the mix of people who lived there, not just transients like Mark and me, but a solid body of settlers, and in particular its 'characters', some of them vividly described in the Horizon piece. 'Vesey' – Dr. Desmond Vesey Fitzgerald was a world renowned natural scientist who had retired from his work with Red Locust Control but still lived by the shores of Lake Chila. His presence, to quote *Abercornucopia* of that time, was an important attraction to numbers of natural scientists studying every aspect of African wild life, flora and entomology. I remember peering into his nocturnal insect-catcher, his naming last night's catches, his additions to the long list of birds spotted in the area and updated in *Abercornucopia*. I was needlessly in awe of him, particularly when, later, I rashly agreed to become Hon. Sec. of the Club, with him as Chairman. He, for the moment, was staying.

There was 'Westy' Westwood, whose business interests spanned the general trading store and butchery, the Abercorn Arms and an estate which included the Lake View Hotel – soon to be sold and turned into Outward Bound Trust's base in Zambia. Genial Ted Davies, behind the bar at the Abercorn Arms, would regale newcomers like us with Abercorn tales from way back: one included the sighting of a London Green Line bus driving through the town, presumably on a Cape to Cairo run. John Carlin at the Lake Press, stout and greying in his safari suit, was always good for a humourous anecdote, many of which would appear in his monthly paper *Abercornucopia*. I soon sensed how much he enjoyed being diverted from his work when I called in, often with Paul in tow, to prop myself on the counter for a chat, then dashing off an aerogramme to catch the plane, in a way Mum would have been proud of. Later I would be tasked with writing up pieces on the doings at the club for the paper, and would feed him snippets of amusing gossip, some of which found their way into his Chila Chat column by 'Impulumushi'. John's wife Sheelagh

John Carlin outside the Lake Press; Abercorn's humour personified

ran the Abercorn Customs Office and his sister Joan was the local Central African Airways rep. Son Colin, recently returned from a stint at London's College of Printing, worked with his father at the Lake Press; he was a keen sailor and one of Abercorn's bachelors, for whom the company of any single young women was almost never available.

Some of its most notable residents had arrived by accident: Derrick Peachey had crash-landed during an air race from Portsmouth to Johannesburg in 1936. Badly injured, he was transferred south and ultimately back to England, but a couple of years later returned to see what could be salvaged from the wreckage of the plane. He married Elaine and they were still fruit farming there on a large estate with ten Doberman Pinscher dogs, known fearfully by his workforce as 'the leopards'.

There was Mary Richards, whose passion was botany. Although already in her late 70's, she would arrive from her other home in Wales each winter and take off into the bush on plant hunting trips with only her driver Ali and an assistant, Abdullah, for company. Though devoted to her, they reputedly found her exhausting company. She would reappear some weeks later with specimens which she would send to Kew Gardens Herbarium – some 20,000 of them over the years. The following year would see her made a Master of Science at the University of Wales for her work.

Most celebrated locally were the Misses Gamwell – known to all as the Gamwell Sisters. Hope and Marion had served in the First Aid Nursing Yeomanry (F.A.N.Y.) as ambulance drivers in World War I. By 1929, in search of a new life in Southern Rhodesia, they were driving from Nairobi to Salisbury and stopped off in Abercorn for supplies. They were offered hospitality over Christmas and never left. They owned an estate of nearly 1000 acres off the Mpulungu road, a fine English-style flower garden complete with sundial and a magnificent 1928 Chevrolet nicknamed 'The Horse' for driving round the estate. In town they were instantly recognisable: two stocky figures in khaki bush jackets and trousers, with cropped grey hair, Bowie knives at the ready in their belts. There was already talk of their leaving, uncomfortable at their increasing dependence on a local workforce they felt was becoming unreliable.

However, we made friends mainly with more recent arrivals of our age. On our little road lived two keen bridge playing couples: IRLCS pilots Robin Crosse-Upcott with his wife Pam, and Ted and Halina Malujlo whose young sons learned Polish first, English second. Gavin Barr was the District Commissioner and a mean guitar player, he and his wife Caroline both radiating Scottish cheerfulness. I remember Caroline's serene smile above the clamour of their three young children and their delinquent lurcher-type dog Bill Barr (we all had large dogs and outdoor social occasions were frequently interrupted by outbreaks of fighting). Tom and Maureen Williamson too had young children: he was our chief of police who seemed to me a slightly stern figure, while she was a kind, calm young mum and a reassuring presence, particularly once I had two young children. And of course there were the Bowmakers, Jennifer (whom we now knew as Jiff) and Alan, who were to become our closest friends. He was a marine biologist and provincial fisheries officer, passionate about animals, easy and affectionate with children, and with a mad, infectious laugh. Jiff was now pregnant again, three months behind me, their one year old Jeanne and Paul firm friends. Their garden I remember as full of livestock – chickens, ducks, cages of rabbits, cats with a new litter. Alan, like Mark, was often away on fisheries matters on Lake Tanganyika; he had the much coveted use of a splendid motor launch the *Dame des Iles*, and of a high-speed launch too. Jiff was a huge support to me, a more confident mum than I, always cheerful and positive, ready with common sense advice. They were both keen sailors. There were many other new friends – too many to mention here – all sociable and agreeable company.

How important these friendships were in a small, isolated community! I remember vividly, early on in our friendship, the experience of some silly falling-out with Jiff – remember it chiefly for the sense of panic and abandonment that overcame me when she would not speak to me, the relief that flooded over me as we made it up. We were all dependent on each other's support: a young mum's necessary trip to the Copper Belt,

125

with all the travelling that this entailed, a sudden illness or even a few days in hospital whilst a husband was away, meant the need for someone else to look after an extra baby or toddler for several days – help always willingly given.

Now, after several months settling in, Mark and I had started to plan my own trip to the Copper Belt, which needed the company's permission. It involved a two day drive down in the company car, Mark returning with a sales colleague while I would stay on for two days of shopping, dentist, blood tests and a gynaecological appointment. Reluctantly, I realised it would be impossible to take Paul, not least because no-one with a cot had invited me to stay (though happily my old Salisbury mate Barbara now lived in nearby Ndola and had a spare sofa). The Bowmakers offered to have him, along with Uelo to help. My letter before we left gives a flavour of how life was developing:

Rather in haste now, as we leave early tomorrow, and there seems to be a lot to think of what with Paul's luggage and Boy going to stay with the Jones's (our neighbours and great dog lovers)… We had a busy weekend, Mark playing golf on Sat. and Sun. a.m. for the Abercorn Open (he did very badly) and then having to go to Mpulungu on Sun. p.m. and Monday for the Liemba. Meanwhile I was preparing for my lunch at the yacht club on Sunday. Dido Millar helped me make pizza pie for 50, plus salad, rolls etc. All the Kasama visitors and golfers came. We charged 2/6 and made £2/10 profit for the club which was very good, and it seemed to go off alright. On Mon. there was special lunch at the main club for the golfers and I made a pudding for that, and Paul and I ate there, Mark arriving later. We had a game of golf later, Mark still playing badly and I not so bad, considering my figure – I am just about in smocks now. I also did lots of gardening over the w/e and am beginning to be rewarded. We had our first decent rain on thurs. with a terrific wind – yachts overturned, boughs broken etc. but it was over too quickly and very hot again now. It will be worse in Ndola. I have a shopping list a mile long.

I remember little of the trip other than my anxiety at leaving Paul, despite knowing how at home he would be with his friend Jeanne and

Paul with Uelo in the front garden...

...and with his friend Jeanne Bowmaker at the Yacht Club

adults he now knew quite well. There was even a concrete paddling pool which had been built for a pet otter which hadn't arrived. We gave him a new car and then we were off: *650 miles of straight road with trees on either side, completely unvarying for the entire journey. I shopped as quickly as possible from my mile long list and did manage to get most of the things I wanted to pack into Mark's car, from garden lime to Christmas presents.* There followed two days of dentist, doctor, blood tests and a hair cut and perm (*the girl didn't even know I was pregnant!*) and some time to feel almost a single girl again with Barbara before flying home.

The greatest thrill was to get back to my little boy: *Paul was struck dumb to see me arrive off the plane,* I wrote home, *but has been so good since, not at all clingy or whining as I had feared... Uelo came every day and Paul dotes on him.*

Despite being nearly seven months pregnant, and having been ordered to rest after a scare with contractions following a gastric upset, my breathless air letters continue to recount endless activity, including a major garden restructuring. This involved Mark learning to operate the Agriculture Department's small motor plough to plough up the front drive, the relocation of the garage '*near to the back door instead of miles from any door at all, by Uelo and a temporary helper at 3/- a day*'. Later I reported making five trips in the Mini with Uelo to fetch rocks, to create a rockery where the new lawn was terraced to cope with a change in level. It was early November and the rains had started with a vengeance, with a dramatic build-up of cumulus thunderheads, forked lightning and heavy tropical downpours, all far more dramatic than we had been used to in Southern Rhodesia. Everyone seemed to have a rain gauge, and that month 11 inches was recorded, one inch falling in a day. Abercorn could receive 50 – 60 inches in a season, even more down towards Lake Tanganyika. By January we were to realise that the rainy season, 'summer', was cooler here than 'winter', with those heavier rains and higher winds than we had been used to and relatively little sun to warm us up. For Paul all this rain was simply an opportunity to go out in his new red Wellingtons, whilst Mark had to cope with increasingly muddy and at times impassable roads, erratic oil tanker deliveries and irate customers waiting for their orders.

Indoors, as well as my other sewing, I was now requesting scraps of material from Mum as *I have started a patchwork quilt for our double bed.* At least, I think now, I must have been sitting down to work on that. To add to it all, I was now on my second house servant, Edward, my discomfort with Daudi having led to some final falling out. I don't remember Edward at all, save for the following incident:

I am sans domestique. Edward was suspected of lying and pinching food, and then I found him (at 11.30 a.m.) in Paul's room lying on the bed. Ugh. He pretended to be ill, but though a born actor, I was too angry to be deceived further. The only applicants so far have been quite hopeless and I'd rather go it alone and try to find someone decent tho it may be difficult. Uelo is a help and can iron nappies and do floors etc so it's not too bad. (It is a tribute to all that ironing over the years that no putse fly ever burrowed its way into our babies' or our flesh.)

I had been told in Ndola that it would be safe for me to have the baby in Abercorn provided that regular blood tests – the samples had to catch the plane to Kitwe for analysis – did not show a build-up of antibodies that would threaten the baby. However, with impeccable timing, our Medical Officer, Chris Roberts was about to go on long leave. He came to stay for a few days while his house was got ready for his locum, Dr. Trant: *She is a dear old girl of about 80 who practises in Tanganyika and was here before Chris. She has a monkey and is deaf but everyone says she's v. good and adores delivering babies. We have ordered a lighter pram which should be here soon. Needless to say names have not been discussed yet, we always disagree anyway.*

I wish I could say that I remember being attended by a doctor with a monkey on her shoulder – but I can't, because of course she left the monkey at home. (It was in fact a bad tempered baboon called Audrey, much disliked in the community; it was diabetic and had to be injected regularly with insulin). Dr Trant was a delightful, feisty old lady, Anglo-Irish and very excited at the prospect of delivering a white baby (there were many black ones arriving in the location hospital, but only mine expected in the European community). My due date was only a couple of weeks before her locum ended, and she was reassuringly determined that I should be delivered before she left.

News of the outside world seldom intrudes into my letters, the last time having been a mention of the Cuba crisis from Gwelo. Now, in early December, between thanks for the Christmas cake in its Tupperware, a list of Paul's new vocabulary and a diagram of the new lawn and rockery, came: *We were horrified about Kennedy, and only heard when I went to the shops on Sat. a.m. & someone said wasn't it awful and I said what was? I even bought all the newspapers the next week. The way it struck me was poor Jacqueline, I kept thinking how she must feel.*

We had no radio, and newspapers were inevitably out of date by the time they were available which was somewhat of a turn-off, together with their expense against our very limited budget. Perhaps too the outside world felt even more remote than it had in Gwelo, immersed as we now were in Abercorn life. Decades later I still come across a political event, a pop song, a book that made a stir, in a documentary looking back at the sixties, and realise how much of it passed me by.

The run-up to Christmas was as hectic as it always is everywhere, the succession of cool damp days, often with a fine mist, reminding me of long ago summer holidays in the Lake District with our Watson grandparents. There were endless company visitors to be entertained; farewell parties at the Club for government people leaving for good; Will to be fetched by Mark from Mpika, after his spell working in Lusaka and on a tourist 'walkabout' including Southern Rhodesia. I checked through my Christmas card list, placed orders with the Army & Navy Stores in London of gifts for family (what did I choose for them? I wonder now, for my letters of course concealed my choices). As I addressed cards to Bulawayo and Gwelo, enclosing a few lines of our news to our friends there, they already seemed far away, so immersed had I become in our new life.

We were all delighted to have Will back for Christmas. Whilst working in Lusaka he had taught himself to cook with a Philip Harben paperback; that and his British upbringing had left him well equipped to help in the house in my servant-less state. I was simultaneously relieved not to have someone in the house whom I did not get on with, and aware that I must have someone installed by the time the babe arrived. Christmas itself brought more drinks parties, a Christmas dinner cooked by Will and me and a visit from the Bowmakers, who having decided that our household had too few animals, arrived triumphantly with Paul's Christmas gift – one of their kittens, called Minnie. Paul adored it and promptly called it Micky – a prescient move as it turned out to be male and required neutering!

New Year proved even more of a whirl than our family Christmas: *We went to the N Y Eve dance at the club and to drinks first with the Malujlos & there was a half hour panto 'Abercornella' quite amusing and topical. Come midnight I've never seen so many people embracing each other, all quite mad.*

The smallest competitor in the longest drive competition

It was a Scottish nicht, with reels, a bagpipe & a super dinner of soup, oatmeal herrings and haggis & we got to bed at 2. Yesterday (a holiday here) we went for a long row on the lake, then to the club at midday for the 'longest drive' competition (golf) which Mark <u>won</u> with a terrific shot! Even little Paul took his turn, hands well down the shaft of an adult-sized driver.

As the January rains continued, a new houseboy, Bourdillon, started; I was initially *'not optimistic'*, but later reported that he was *'quite good'*. Will returned to England and his Foreign Office exams, and I began to hope that this time the baby wouldn't be late – well, later than the date I had been given. Blood tests being clear of antibodies, I could plan for an Abercorn delivery. Dear Dr. Trant had pronounced herself an authority on determining the sex of the unborn infant – by its heart beat – and after earnestly listening to my tum, had confidently pronounced it another boy. Of course we tried not to mind, but I wrote home *'oh dear, goodbye Caroline then, I must hope I can avoid it being dull 'John'…'* Mark, in a Christmas thank you letter, tried valiantly to be even-handed: *I am sure you would like a grand-daughter, but most of the money seems to be on its being a boy, but I hope the punters are dumbfounded. Still we shall be pleased with whatever we get.*

My letters, so preoccupied with my late pregnancy, make no mention of the January elections that would lead to self-government later in the year. Kenneth Kaunda's United National Independence Party (UNIP) won 55 of the 65 seats, and he was sworn in as prime minister with an entirely African cabinet. Northern Rhodesia was on the last leg of its journey to independence.

Calling Barbara Yates

Now and then I have another look
for my old address book, try to visualise
your entry – though I know it wouldn't do,
even the country's changed its name
and you and I moved on. So I am left
with your crazy laugh over yet more beer,
that night spent on your knobbly couch, and how
you got me, hangover and all, to the old airport
just in time for check-in. Sometimes I wonder
if your name's out there in cyberspace
waiting for me to find you.

CHAPTER 10

Nuns' head-dresses 'fluttering like great white birds'

The government Land Rover lurched and bumped its way down the road to Mpulungu. 'Faster!' I urged, hanging on for dear life. Alan had offered to take me on a birth-inducing trip down to the fisheries on the lake, for this baby too was late, Mark was needed at the Abercorn depot and I, large and hot, was fed up.

The rough drive was to no avail. However, this time my doctor was my ally, for Dr Trant's locum stint was coming to an end, and, anxious not to miss this baby, she insisted I was ready for an induction. I happily agreed, Paul went to stay with the McLoughlins and his friend Pip, and I checked into the little bungalow hospital under the care of Sister Amabilis. From there, on 6 February 1964, Mark wrote one of his rare letters, to be taken by a colleague leaving next day and posted on the Copper Belt: it is headed 'The Labour Ward': ... *she is now in full labour and we hope that in a few hours we shall have a bonny baby with us. Amanda is fine and appears to be enjoying herself really. She is looking very pretty and I am sure that everything will be alright ...the Bowmakers have visited several times and Pix*

McLoughlin (looking after Paul)... we thought you would love to have the latest up to date news from your man on the spot.

I am astonished to read that I was looking very pretty, and enjoying myself. But yes, how much easier it was second time around! By sundowner time Mark had been despatched to wait elsewhere, as husbands were in those days, and drank gin with the Bowmakers next door. I remember the nuns' headdresses fluttering around me like great white birds, their encouraging Irish voices, Dr Trant's warm tones, and the sudden realisation in the midst of my hard work that my baby had indeed arrived. Then came Dr Trant's surprised 'Oh! It's a wee girlie!'. Our daughter Caroline had slipped easily into the world, and Mark and I had our longed for 'pigeon pair'.

Mark came in and saw her half an hour later, then was off to celebrate with company colleagues up on a visit. Next morning at the depot his clerk greeted the news with a wide smile and 'Ah – another little Zambian has arrived!'. Mark despatched telegrams, but it was another five days before I could catch the mail plane with an account of the whole thing to her grandparents. How different the regime from stern old Birchenough House in Gwelo! The baby was in a cot by my bed during the day, though removed at night so that I could sleep, and : '*This is the hospital to be in – no visiting hours, coffee provided for visitors, and Mark drops in at all hours. People here are so kind – I had masses of flowers, and presents. There are two sisters on duty, one day and one night, very Irish and amusing – they are blood sisters. They all adore babies and nothing is too much trouble for Caroline, nor for dear old Dr Trant, who leaves on Thursday, when Chris is due back. However I am going home tomorrow, I wouldn't go so early but Mark is taking a few days leave from today to the w/e, so he can help out while I get a bit organised. I am apprehensive at having to manage a baby and Paul. Paul all this time has been with the McLoughlin's and his girlfriend Pip. It is reported they are getting on alright, but I've only seen him twice, over the w/e with Mark, as it seemed to upset him afterwards. He was most intrigued to hear cries coming from a cot, and had to have a good look, but lost interest after a while as she wasn't much value for playing with!*

There were three sisters: Amabilis and Romana who were blood sisters, and a novice Sister Lazalet. They were great fun and I remember their

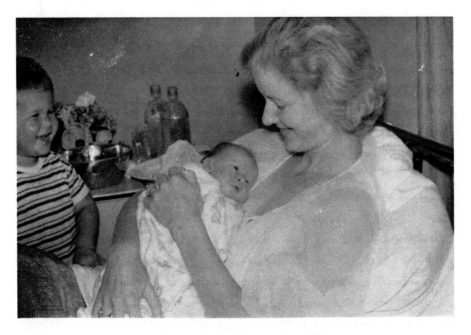

In hospital: Caroline at 3 days old

pride at the recent promotion of a cousin to Cardinal. Hospital was a happy time for me, although I feel sad now, realising how little access Paul had to his mum; that is another thing that would not happen today. Caroline's first days were well recorded on camera (in contrast to Paul's, our earliest of him being at several weeks old), for Pix McLoughlin was a keen photographer who also did her own developing and printing. Paul, snapped sitting on my bed with the baby, looks by turns happy and slightly bewildered, as indeed he must have been. I was anxious about going home to cope with two small children, especially as our servant at that time, Bourdillon, did no cooking – '*tins will no doubt come in*' – and worried – '*I do hope Paul's not going to be jealous of the attention he'll inevitably lose, and we shall have to try to spend plenty of time on him to start with. He's sure to want to wheel the pram all day!*'

The first weeks at home were not easy: poor Paul was miserable and whiney, we assumed as a reaction to his stay away, but he turned out to be cutting all four back teeth at once, the effects enhanced by a nasty cold. He mizzled all day and woke at night, whilst I had 'post partum neuralgia' up my neck and into my head, and of all things, a boil on my bottom. Thank heavens Mark was on what we now call paternity leave. In the midst of this, baby Caroline settled in quite happily: *Your granddaughter is fine and really no trouble at all. One does enjoy a second baby so much more that the first. I don't worry about crying etc. and find everything easier this time. The feeding continues well and I consume vast quantities of beer and food, and try to rest, as I am determined not to fail now.* Paul soon learned to pat 'baba' on the back for winding, carrying nappies to the soak bucket and dashing at the pram with a dummy at the first cry, (this last much to my mother's dismay, for to her dummies were 'common' and to be avoided at all costs). By the time Mark went back to work, Paul was a real daddy's boy, with a sad 'Dad's away' during his many business trips.

I was determined to keep on with breastfeeding. I can remember Jiff and I bending over the pram in the garden, her finger stroking the baby's cheek: Look how well she is on it! she exclaimed. And she was. But other elements of life militated against my avowed regime of a quiet life with plenty of rest, of spending time not only with my baby, but with my little boy, who was having to adjust to not being the only child in the family.

For a start there was my now much loved gardening. It was so easy to achieve the rapid results I craved, so satisfying, so hard to put off! With impeccable timing, the dozen rose bushes I had ordered from Ndola had arrived, bare rooted, as I came out of hospital. In they must go straight away, into the new island beds around the freshly planted kikuyu grass lawn, lightly shaded by a couple of miombo trees: white Iceberg (still a favourite everywhere), deep red fragrant Papa Meilland, vivid flaming Super Star, Eclipse, Brazil, Largo … no colour coordination, just lots of colour. Practical Jiff was asking, Why all these flowers? What you need is a bigger veg patch! She was right of course, and in that climate, with the help of plenty of fertiliser, you could grow pretty much anything, and quickly too. Later we raised everything from spinach to aubergines, but for now, determined to have my English garden, it was flowers I craved; my carnations raised from seed were blooming, and trays of delicate annuals like linaria and mignonette were coming on, to go at the feet of the roses. Soon I was into *'a spate of winter planting, sweet peas, dahlias, a huge bed of arum lilies etc. – then to start the new veg. garden. We shared a truckload of manure with the Bowmakers. She has smocked a beautiful little dress for Caroline'*. By mid-year I was able to write: ' *In a vase today I have lupins, sweet peas, carnations, chrysanths, petunias and a large rose, all grown by me. Super broad beans and broccoli too.'*

But the principal reason I could not sit at home, leading a quiet, baby-focussed life was the lure of Abercorn's club and lively social activities. It tapped into that old, deep need to be at the centre of things, to be popular, above all never to be left out. Hating the thought of things taking place without me, I was always a ready volunteer, certain that I could combine all this busy-ness with being a good wife and mother, giving my children all the attention they needed. I feel sad about that now, even as I remember what tremendous fun we had too. By mid- March I was writing to my parents: *A v. good day's sailing on Sunday, all day, and I have begun taking the tiller again. I can feed Caroline in the ladies' loo. It's 40 for lunch every week now, and I shall have to do it again soon. I am Yacht Club gardener and must go and do some this p.m. Now Pix wants me to take over as Main Club Secretary, I'm not sure if I have time. Committee meetings, once a month, are 5.30 pm, which is hopeless, but they might change the time.* However, in the same letter I had already reported: *Caroline is fine, but a slow gainer compared to Paul, only 3 oz this week, now 7lb 9 oz. I hope she's getting enough!* There was a sad inevitability in my writing in early April that she was now bottle fed – *'having so much to do didn't help'.*

Social life in Abercorn had a momentum of its own, and with Easter's approach I reported that regardless of Holy Week, life was *'quite frantic. Last Sat. the doctor gave an absolute bunfight sundowner and we gave the Bowmakers fish and chips at 10.30 pm. Sailing all Sunday. Out to dinner last night, again tonight, then a frantic Easter w/e. A friend of Mark's from Kasama plus fiancée are staying Sat. night. All Sat. and Mon. are our big Regatta, with lunch and an evening braaivleis there on Sat. and lunch again on Monday, which I am doing with the vet's wife and we are catering for 60. A fish thing in big baking trays and salad. On top of that we've decided to give a fondue party on Sun. night, which has swelled to 11. It's meat fondue, you dip pieces of fillet steak in deep hot oil and then into a dish of various sauces. Mark got hold of a Bunsen burner as oil heater, and we flew the steak up from Ndola. Road transport has been so bad, with terrible rains recently, that even the refrigerated truck arrives with the meat rotten. I've also had to do ghastly things like washing loose covers and making a Christening cake, wh. I hope someone else will ice!*

All this plus 2 kids is a bit much, but fortunately isn't for long! Caroline seems to need feeding 3-hourly during the day, as she can't hold a lot at one sitting, but is doing well, 7lbs 15 oz today, and laps up cereal at 6 pm. She smiles a lot and looks older and more human. Paul is fine though seems poor thing to have a genius for doing things he oughtn't.

With the wisdom of hindsight I now realise that, probably like most babies at that time, Caroline was started on solid foods far too early, when what her immature digestion needed was six months of plenty of milk. Perhaps as a result, she went through several months of gastric upsets, on one occasion spending two nights in hospital with severe diarrhoea, and I continued for some months to report that, despite being a very active and happy baby, she ate 'like a little bird'.

I remember the fun of that first meat fondue vividly: the recipe came from, of all sources, Playboy magazine (of which more later). You provided at least three dipping sauces, including my first shot at hollandaise and it was a huge success. I loved cooking – still do – and that letter also reminds me of something else that kept many of us busy – the amount of cooking we did; large-scale catering for the club and frequent entertaining were something we all learned as we went along. Nothing fancy, mostly: for the sailing club the 'fish thing' I had mentioned was portions of Lake Tanganyika nile perch tray-baked in a tomato sauce; other times, huge 'pizza pies' or pasta dishes, so unauthentic that Giuseppe, Abercorn's unofficial barber, whose day job was managing the local flour mill, refused to come for lunch on our 'Italian' days. Entertaining at home ranged from stretching whatever we were having with pasta or local rice (grown down at Mpulungu), through to carefully planned meals with meat – there was always meat (pre-ordered) and vegetables from the garden. Braaivleis were usually big affairs at the club, rather than at home, like the whole buck roasted for a club 'do' to say farewell to a number of departing couples. And who could forget Mrs. Campbell-Gray's Sunday curry lunches? Redolent of the days of the Raj (for she had lived in India), they were surrounded by a huge array of side dishes from toasted coconut to fried onion slices to chopped peppers. I still have her recipe for chicken curry, which includes tomatoes, a can of evaporated milk and curry powder, which you add to the hot oil 'judging the amount by eye' as she mysteriously advises.

And where were all our children during this constant whirl of social activity, you might well ask? The quick answer is that they were almost always wherever we mums were: playing in the garden mostly, kept an eye on by a garden boy, as we cooked; in little playgroups in our houses when we met to plan a club event or sew; around us in larger groups at the club house or, better still from their point of view, on the shores of Lake Chila at the Yacht Club. They all knew each other well, shared their toys and generally had a happy, largely outdoor life. In the evenings we either took them with us, asleep in the car, popping out regularly to see them, or babysat for each other. Almost all domestic servants were men and it was not deemed advisable to leave children at home with them. Our little Mini estate made a good-sized dormitory for Paul in a sleeping bag and Caroline in her carry cot, although later, when she took to clambering out, we relied more on baby sitters and did resort occasionally to leaving them with the trusted Uelo.

Into this whirl of activity came Mark's parents for a fortnight's visit, their chance to meet their grand-daughter and for 'Boompapa' to see Paul for the first time since he was tiny. The timing also meant they could be there for Caroline's Christening. They arrived bearing toys, baby dresses and even clothes for me. Despite being the opposite of me in build, Mother was brilliant at choosing things that suited me – a welcome talent for a daughter-in-law so far from any clothes shops. Invitations to drinks and dinners came thick and fast; we took them on our only tourist trails –

Mpulungu and the Liemba, and the Kalambo Falls – played bridge, and prepared for the Christening party. By dint of much pestering we had persuaded the Archdeacon to visit Abercorn, and on Sunday 12 April, after the 4 p.m. service in the little church decorated with Mother's flower arrangements, about 35 guests and their children came home for tea, cake and champagne cocktails. Standing on our front terrace – the rains having now finished – I felt proud of our new garden with its green lawn and the rose bushes already starting to bloom. Photos show our smart guests glass in hand, all the men in suits, the women in frocks and hats and Jiff, Caroline's godmother, elegant in pale, elbow-length gloves. Someone had indeed iced the cake, for a close-up photo by Pix in Caroline's baby book shows an elaborate riot of roses and trellis patterns in white icing, topped by the stork from Paul's Christening cake. Perhaps it was done by Mrs.

With the Cape Town grandparents at Caroline's Christening

Smit, a show prize-winner, whose cake for the 10th anniversary celebrations of All Saints' Church had been '*a masterpiece of confectionery bearing on its iced surface a sugar model of the church building, perfectly executed and much admired by everyone*', as *Abercornucopia* had reported.

The grandparents' departure left that sad quiet gap that follows any successful visit: Paul missed all the attention, I Mother's practical help and even Boy had got used to regular grooming and walkies. Mark though had to catch up with work after his holiday, and his spirits were low. The relentless pressure of covering a very large sales area, of having to look after numerous visitors (the depot on Lake Tanganyika a constant source of interest), and of feeling he was not being kept up-to-date with company matters were getting him down. And holiday or no, the S.S. Liemba must be met, every other Sunday.

Caroline with her Dad at one month

Paul baby-minding

It was at about this time that the Liemba brought another mini-drama to Abercorn: a young girl travelling down from Kigoma turned out to have smallpox. There was an instant alert and Caroline for one had to have her inoculation far earlier than had been planned. I remember Chris Roberts showing us a photo of the child, her impassive face and skinny body a mass of raised pustules. I must have realised how much it would have worried my parents, for – atypically – I discreetly left this news item out of my letters home.

I was now busy with staff training, having sacked Bourdillon in exasperation after some last misdemeanour. Jiff matter-of-factly explained to me that by now I would have a poor reputation with any available local workforce as an impatient "cheeky madam". Why not, she suggested, train up Uelo, whom I got on with and who was bright enough to learn all I needed? And she and Alan could recommend a piccanin – a young lad I could train up in the garden, who had done some work for them and was keen to learn. It worked a treat; soon Uelo could do *'far more than Bourdillon ever could'* and young Friday was *'a great success in the garden, chasing Paul with the hose while watering, pushing him on his trike and learning to do the endless nappy ironing'*. I remember them both as bright, cheerful lads, always good-tempered and, like Daniel, able to deflect my impatience with reassuring smiles.

We had now been in Abercorn a year, felt settled in the little community, where we had made good friends. How fortunate we were, I think now, to have lived in that small but vivid world at that particular time! We wives and mothers especially, unencumbered by much in the way of domestic chores, could pursue whatever projects we fancied, our children playing together as we socialised. The club, still largely unaffected by the forthcoming prospect of multi-racial membership, flourished. Mark was now chairman of the golf section, playing well and busy organising matches with visiting teams. I was now secretary of the main club and active in the yacht section: with two children I had had to give up any pretence of being a golfer, but with the yacht club's safe play area for children, and friends to keep an eye on Caroline in her carrycot, I now felt I could give free rein to my recently developed passion for sailing. I loved everything about it: the excitement of hanging out by your toes in the teeth of a high wind, pushing the boat to its limits, the rush of activity at 'Ready about! – lee-o!', the boom swinging over and the scramble to trim the sails. On quieter days, inching the boat along in the lightest of breezes, you had time to chat with your sailing partner, to notice your shoulders burning and wish you had put on a shirt over your bikini, to hear other voices across the water, a snatch of a Bob Dylan song *blowing in the wind* perhaps, or a burst of laughter. I surprised myself with my competitive streak, the low cunning I could employ to steal another boat's wind when the breeze died. Competitive sailing took place on Sundays, so that Mark missed every alternate one, but at the club we minded each others' children, took turns to skipper and crew, the wives to produce lunch. As well as couples with young families there were also agreeable bachelors about, including smiling Colin Carlin who always seemed to be around, ready as a sailing partner or to lend the little boat he had built. To have the little lake, spring-fed and free from the liver fluke that caused the debilitating disease bilharzia, to have the use of the dinghies, Enterprises and Graduates mostly, free with club membership – what extraordinary good fortune! (Much later I watched sailing on an

144

English midlands reservoir, saw how cold it was, learned how expensive, and sensed that my sailing days were over). There was the on-going fun of a social life with a wide variety of friends, mostly our age with young families. (I say 'variety', but of course all of them were white – European, as we called ourselves, although many had never lived in Europe, or not for decades.) Life, at least on the surface, was busy and enjoyable.

Fun, busy, enjoyable – yes, life was all of those things, but as in any marriage other factors were also in play. There were the pressures of Mark's job, which not only took him away so much, but was also far from head

Hon. Sec. Abercorn Club, photo courtesy Horizon magazine, where it was captioned: *Amanda L – , secretary of Abercorn Club, and leading member of its yacht section, believes that Abercorn has it all. 'You just cannot be bored here' she says.*

office and which became increasingly burdensome to him. I felt sympathetic but helpless as he complained about the lack of support, and how this meant he had to be always sending telegrams, phoning (not easy, lines were often down) and even writing – never his strong suit. At the same time we were frequently inundated with visitors and the need to entertain them. I can see now the resulting stress affected our respective health in different ways.

Mark could not sleep and was *'drinking more than is good for him'* as I put it in a letter home. Fortunately our doctor, Chris, managed to convince him to cut down his drinking, and to get exercise, but Mark would not allow him to request the company to let him have sick leave, which would certainly have led to a black mark on his file. I meanwhile was coping with the unwelcome re-emergence of my 'bad back' problem – a traumatic development for me, given the surgery I had had aged 19, and my memories of the way it had put my life on hold. It first 'went' while Mark was on a 10 day stint at Head Office on a course (*'too much lifting while he was away – no more lifting ever again'*, I wrote, unrealistically.) At first I tried a borrowed infrared lamp for strained sacro-iliac muscles. As the pain became more acute Chris offered me bed rest, which I felt was impossible, or a plaster cast to keep me from bending. This last proved both uncomfortable and entirely ineffective. There were of course no local services like physiotherapy, no Pilates exercise classes or chiropractic, which have helped me so much in recent years. Eventually, and distinctly unwillingly, the company agreed to arrange for me to see the only orthopaedic surgeon of any repute, who was down in Salisbury – a lengthy trip which would have meant leaving the children for some days. I postponed this, hobbled along trying unsuccessfully to do less, finally managing to order by mail from the Copper Belt a support corset, which helped enough for me to decide not to press for the Salisbury trip. I learned, many years later, the extent to which my back could 'go' as an expression of my need for greater support somewhere in my life. Then of course I was just a young wife and mum worrying about my husband, determined to keep things going at home and, being me, wanting to be part of whatever was going on in the community.

Woman's Own, 1964

The oven's on as low as it will go,
children asleep. She glances at her watch.
Soon surely? She flips a magazine.

In between *The Perfect Pedicure*
and *Casseroles for Chilly Days*, she's drifted
to Kensington, the basement flat she shared

with friends. They'd window shop the Brompton Road,
full skirts swishing over net petticoats,
in short white gloves. They'd pass around the latest

hags' mags, Woman's Own or Woman, read
them on the tube. Last thing she'd settle in
with the short stories, four per issue, lost

in fragile love first glimpsed as pulses raced,
in heart stopping quarrels and misunderstandings,
chewing a nail until at last a head

could rest on a tweedy shoulder. Better yet,
he'd cup a tearful face between strong hands
and breathe, 'I love you – you are all I need'.

Crunch of tyres on gravel, headlights rake
the curtains. Thank God. She spoons stew onto plates,
pictures a Saturday picnic by the lake
till he calls: *The golf match starts at eight.*

CHAPTER 11

Of high-kicking bunny girls, and a clarinet unpacked

By now the pace of change was accelerating, with independence only a few months off. Soon after Africa Freedom Day came the company's demand that Mark organise a multi-racial cocktail party during a visit from the Chairman: *About 20 people, we are instructed. Trouble is there are v. few Africans here important or civilised enough to ask, but it is to keep the 2 clerks company, and one of the chaps from Tanganyika is I think Indian or something … the company's Tanganyika G.M. is also coming – they are obviously going to consult at Mpulungu on petrol supplies – M. is going to have to hire a bus to get them down there.* We racked our brains for local Africans to invite, and John Carlin at the Lake Press printed little invitations, offering to attend himself 'as an ancient monument of local interest'. As I welcomed them – mostly men who had chosen to come without their wives – I felt awkward and inhibited, for I had never socialised with Africans. I could chat up the company chairman with ease, but these men, for me, came from some unknown world and I had no idea where to start. I watched friends whose daily lives in government service or in business involved mixing with Africans at all levels, saw them comfortably chatting and joking with them. I envied but did not know how to emulate them. Still, the party and the trip to Mpulungu seemed to go off well enough for Mark to feel he had earned some brownie points with the big boss.

In our local paper, 'Cornelius' – the name always reminded me of the wise old elephant in the *Babar* children's books – now ruminated on issues such as the wisdom of a stand-alone currency for the country based only on copper and its unpredictable market fluctuations. My letters continued to grumble about deteriorating postal services (though not our local Post Office, run most efficiently by its new African manager), and of how shops no longer catered for Europeans. The Gamwell sisters had put their estate, Chilongolwelo, on the market – a great blow as they were such significant figures in our little community – and one by one, couples who were our good friends were selling off unwanted possessions and heading back to Europe or elsewhere. For many others there was the likelihood, or at least the possibility, of their jobs being 'Zambianised'. We busied ourselves with sailing, bridge evenings, supper with friends, the respective sections of the club setting up competitions and tournaments. But change and uncertainty permeated all our conversations.

No matter: as if in a communal act of insouciance against all these winds of change, the yacht section of the club now planned its biggest fundraising event ever – the Commodore's Ball, for it needed funds for the upkeep of the boats. Someone had had the bright idea of writing an appeal to Lord Abercorn in Scotland, after whose forebear, the Chairman of the British South Africa Company who took over its administration in 1895, the town had been named. Not surprisingly this had been unsuccessful. Now we wanted to rival the tennis section's 'grand weekend event' held the previous year, when record sums had been raised at a ball and cabaret.

The star attraction on that occasion had been 'Miss Pamela the Tassel Tosser'. It was rare for a female entertainer to be prepared to come as far as Abercorn, let alone unaccompanied, and word had spread to the furthest outlying homestead, attracting large numbers of single men in the area. Male members not seen for years appeared. To the strains of her taped music (on 'a tape-recording apparatus kindly provided by Mr Marbus of the Electricity Corporation', as our paper reported) Miss Pamela had swayed and twirled, tossing the four long silky tassels attached to her breasts and buttocks. A finale in which tassels fore and aft, right and left, spun in opposite directions had brought a standing ovation from the men, and left us women wondering how on earth she did it (or as our reporter had put it, had 'greatly impressed … especially, it seems, the ladies who particularly appreciated the difficulties she so skilfully overcame'). On our way home Mark and I and Chris Roberts had dropped in at the Bowmakers for a nightcap. While Chris tried to remember his anatomical training and sketched diagrams trying to work out which muscle tweaked where, Jiff and I had shrugged our shoulders and clenched our buttocks and collapsed defeated in fits of laughter.

For the Commodore's Ball we were hoping to sell up to 80 tickets, with the hall and stage decorated *in the style of South Pacific, and supper of a paella – sort of – with salads made by me* I wrote home. The entertainment was to be provided in-house. It was to be a black tie and long frock affair and I got sewing immediately on a strappy number with a swirling long skirt.

Over a four-day bank holiday weekend I had plenty of time, for not only was Mark leading the Abercorn golf team in Kasama, but there was no sailing – at least not in Abercorn. The Bowmakers, Colin C and three other couples had taken four of the dinghies to Broken Hill on the Copper Belt for the national sailing championships. I felt very frustrated that we were not free to go, though much less so when they returned, with accounts of terrific gales, capsizings and two broken masts, not to mention the hardships of chilly, wet camping with young children. But meanwhile a lonely bank holiday weekend loomed for me, till William Winterton suggested I and the children join a party to Lake Tanganyika for the Sunday. William, known as Willum in our household, where Paul was devoted to him, was one of the agreeable young bachelors about the place, on a gap year with V.S.O. and based at Mpulungu, where he spent much of his time building a catamaran out of two canoes. He and others – Colin

Tait in Fisheries, Colin Carlin – were all very pleasant though quite proper company for us young wives whose husbands' jobs took them away, and I suppose we were 'eye candy' for them in the absence of any young single women. When on a couple of occasions Mark and I were hosts to visiting eligible females, we were immediately besieged by eager callers.

Our day out was to be on the government launch the Dame des Iles, which slept five and was comfortable and fast. For once it was not too hot down at the lake level, and eight of us and our children set out for a day of fishing round the islands and a picnic. We even went out to meet the S.S. Liemba as she steamed in, towing her barge of oil products – it was the one and only time that Mark had delegated the task of unloading the barge to his Mpulungu clerk. The word 'lake' is not, for me, adequate to describe that expanse of water so vast as to feel more like a sea. Swimming from the boat in open water was something I never got used to, always aware of the immense depths beneath me, the thousands of feet of 'dead water' far below, filling the bottom of the Great Rift Valley. We did believe, however, that its waters, which tasted sulphurous, were good for bleaching our hair, so I conscientiously wetted and sun-dried mine whenever we were there; never mind the straw texture, the blonder the better. It could be nerve-racking with small children on board, as there often were, for you had to be vigilant every second. So when Colin invited us to go out on the Nancol, an open boat he had bought from the Gamwell sisters, and rigged with a mast and two sails, *'we took advantage of a new Abercorn arrival Jo Bailes, who does babysitting for money: we dropped the kids off, went down to Mpulungu and sailed with a picnic lunch on Lake Tanganyika, swam from the boat, then put on the outboard and followed the Liemba into port ... it all made a fine change from Lake Chila.*

The lake could be dangerous too, with sudden storms and gales whipping up huge waves. For the holiday Tuesday I had planned a curry lunch for twelve and ten children, spending Monday cooking ahead. Half of our guests, though, had gone on another government launch up the lake to a tourist camp, Kasaba Bay, where *'by early Tuesday a terrific gale was blowing – the*

On Lake Tanganyika: Colin Carlin on the Nancol, seeing in the Liemba

On Lake Tanganyika: William Winterton ('Willum') and local fishing boat

'Kapata', a 3-day affair peculiar to July, and due to immense waves they couldn't come back. We didn't realise this till 1 p.m., by which time we had slaved all morning ... what a waste! ... They only finally returned two days later.'

Once the Bowmakers had returned from leave in Salisbury, during which time I was kept busy checking on rabbits and hens, walking dogs and deep-freezing their beans, the committee started preparations for the ball in earnest. It was decided that the cabaret would consist of selected numbers from South Pacific mimed by a male chorus to the soundtrack of the musical, followed by a high-kick routine by a chorus of six bunny girls (*'and if you don't know what they are, ask Will!'* I wrote). I have said in an earlier chapter that Playboy would get another mention: it seems strange to me now, after all the changes in awareness wrought by feminism in the intervening decades, that Playboy magazine was passed around as regular household reading. While I felt vaguely uncomfortable at the pneumatic centrefolds, our husbands enjoyed it for what it was, and I for one, as a good wife, was not going to object and be accused of being a spoilsport. I rationalised madly about its good fiction and other features (witness the meat fondue recipe). And, well, the event and in particular the cabaret turned out to be enormous fun.

A team of six of us wives set to work on our costumes. We were, as you had to be, solution-focussed:

- We've all got Merry Widows, for a start, haven't we? (Of course we did.)
- Hardly decent though, are they?
- But we could add a bit of lacy skirt where the suspenders go...
- Mine's white though, too underwear-ish for a floorshow!
- So's mine – but we can trim the seams with black velvet ribbon ...
- What about collars and cuffs?
- That stiff stuff you use for lining collars and things will do... I've got some.
- ... and very thin foam sheeting to cut ears from, pinched onto alice bands!

- Tails...? I know, big pom-poms made with wool on two circles of cardboard, you know, like we used to make when we were kids!

I should explain for younger readers that a 'Merry Widow' was a 'corselet' produced by Warner lingerie and named after the Strauss operetta – so, think wasp waist and pushed-up bosom, but also metal zip, hooks and eyes, wires and unyielding nylon voile. Lana Turner is quoted as saying: 'I'm telling you, the Merry Widow was designed by a man. A woman would never do that to another woman'.

The all-important white bunny tails were finally sewn on behind – though not too firmly, for we had decided that each bunny would award her tail to a male member who had made a particular contribution to the yacht club, and he would have to snip it off in a prize-giving ceremony to conclude our performance.

Our own costumes complete, all we had to do was to sew white sailor hats for the men to go with their white T shirts and rolled-up white trousers, and the cabaret team was ready – well, apart from a week of nightly rehearsals of course. Mark was to be MC as well as a miming sailor, and I had offered my carnations to make buttonholes to sell to male guests, so with that and the catering it was a particularly busy time.

All the hard work was worth it. I ditched my usual cramped aerogramme and reached for the airmail pad: *The Commodore's Ball was a howling and fantastic success, 91 people (we'd estimated 80 at most). The Bunny Girls (Barbara Mac was Mother Bunny!) were a wow, appearing before supper with carnation buttonholes (55 of them made by <u>me</u>) to sell to the men. Then we dished out supper, paella and salad, garlic bread etc. and puds. The cabaret came straight after, and was fabulous, the men's sailors' mime (Mark was in that) was encored and so was the Bunnies' dance routine. It ended with the awards of Bunnies' tails to various hard workers of the Yacht Club who deserved them! Then the Bunnies and Sailors came down and started the dancing. Lots of photos were taken so I hope to be able to send some. Twisting etc. went on till 4 a.m., with <u>no</u> awful drunks, no lechers pursuing Bunnies or other anticipated horrors! Mark was M.C. and jolly good too. It really was a fabulous do, <u>and</u> made money – and all for 15/- a double ticket.*

Bunny Girls dancing to The Hully Gully
Left to right: Jiff Bowmaker, Chris North, Barbara Mackinson, Glenda Tobin, Pam
Crosse-Upcott, Self

My bunny tail is Alan Bowmaker's award for services to the Yacht Club

There was a heartless P.S. to my account of the event: *Sunday at the Yacht Club was a scream as everyone, except M and I, had the runs from the seafood in the paella!!* I am ashamed to have to reveal that my competitive streak led me to regard this unfortunate catering mishap as an opportunity to win a few races.

Throughout August it seemed as if the pace of change and the pace of our hectic social life went hand in hand. Mike and Liz Rushton, off to run Edinburgh zoo, held a leaving sale, as did the Gamwell Sisters. These sales were, with the shortage of goods in local shops, significant events where you might find just the frock or piece of furniture or ornament you were looking for. Liz came from the USA and I was thrilled to be able to augment my homemade wardrobe with her stylish American cottons. In the case of the Misses Gamwell, everyone, it seemed, wanted some small memento of these two remarkable women, who had contributed so much to the little community over nearly 40 years. I bought a shawl crocheted of wool so gossamer-fine you could pull it through a wedding ring. Their farewell party, with drinks and snacks, speeches and the presentation of gifts was a moving affair. They hoped to drive their 1928 Chevrolet ('The Horse') around South Africa, before sailing from the Cape, from thence planning to live in the Channel Islands. (In the event it turned out to be too complicated to import the car into South Africa, and it was driven back to Abercorn, and thence to a dealer on the Copper Belt, with hopes it would find its way into a museum.) In the same week, there was one of the occasional film shows at the Institute – 'a Peter Sellers film' – a barbecue at the Barrs, ending with a fine guitar session from Gavin, and a party at the Bowmakers on the Rushtons' last night. All this came in the days following one of our particularly energetic weekends: on Saturday, a large party after baby Philip Bowmaker's Christening, where we danced on the verandah to the light of a full moon, going home after bacon and eggs at 3 a.m., only to get up four hours later for a rare Holy Communion service at 8 a.m. with the visiting Archdeacon. Then, as there was a gale blowing, we followed this with an excellent day's sailing; however, Mark was first to capsize, then William, for whom I was crewing, put us in the drink where, treading water under a very wet mainsail, I became convinced I had lost my contact lenses. (Miraculously, I hadn't).

As a reminder of the reality of impending independence, now only a couple of months away, our president-elect Kenneth Kaunda visited Outward Bound's headquarters. On the shores of lake Chila I duly photographed him and his entourage gazing out at the rough waters in the teeth of a gale, Gavin our District Commissioner in attendance. Within a couple of weeks of his visit, Kaunda had become the country's first prime minister. There was another multi-racial sundowner, this time hosted by our District Commissioner, Gavin Barr and Caroline. Perhaps I was getting the hang of things, for I wrote: *I was much amused to chat to up and coming Africans from UNIP [United National Independence Party], the rural district council etc. Their wives sat against the wall in a row with babies. And on Saturday the first Africans who are being put up for membership of the club entered the portals – a historic moment. The first three are good chaps and will get in ok – one is Alan's fish ranger. Independence isn't far off so it's all just as well.*

There is, in one of my letters at this time, a hint of concern about Mark's job. Instead of staying on in Abercorn until the following June (for which we had applied for long leave to go to England), he was to be transferred to Lusaka in March, to a job as yet unspecified. But no more information was forthcoming, and in the meantime both Mark and I were distracted by the delightful prospect of a short holiday. At the Bowmakers' invitation, we were to go by government fisheries boat up the west coast of Lake Tanganyika, past Kasaba Bay tourist camp to spend four or five days at a rest camp at Sumbu. Holidays at that time were almost exclusively taken as 'long leave', for there was, in that remote corner, nowhere easily reached for a short break, other than Kasaba Bay rest camp for lakeside game spotting, which Mark and I could not have afforded anyway. So this was a rare treat, especially as Alan had the government fisheries resources at his disposal:

Alan has to do work up there, Mark is taking some leave and Jiff and I are

Kenneth Kaunda (left), his entourage and Gavin Barr DC (centre)

bringing two children apiece and a lot of food. There is a rest camp there, very good fishing and bathing, and it will mean Mark can really get away from all his worries. We are going in the 'Dame des Iles', a bigger boat than the fisheries launch, it should all be marvellous fun ... We are busy getting in tins of supplies, as there is no fridge at the camp and the only fresh things are fish you catch and chickens. Fortunately the 'Dame des Iles' is equipped with everything + 3 cabins, and we will also have the smaller fisheries launch for short fishing and bathing trips, and another fisheries chap is bringing the Landrover round by road so we can try to shoot some game. It will be pretty hot and I hope to do lots of swimming and sunbathing, and Mark will get a real rest from the company and the phone.

On our return, all looking very tanned and fit, for we had lived in bathing suits, I wrote enthusiastically of our 'marvellous holiday': *We managed to leave the house, clean and locked, at 6 a.m. on Friday and finally left Mpulungu on the 'Dame des Iles' at 8 a.m. – the baggage on the quay looked like a tropical exploration party setting off for 6 months. We spent most*

*of the day getting to Sumbu, with lunch at Kasaba Bay rest camp – no
elephants for once. We only had one of the three rest houses at Sumbu for 2
days, so the Bowmakers slept on board. We had a big bedroom and bathroom,
and front mosquito-netted stoep for eating etc., all v. well ventilated against
the heat, which is pretty terrific. We had 2 boys operating the boat, our 2 house
boys to do washing etc., and the old chap there cooked, when he wasn't drunk,
which was half the time. Then Alan had his small v. fast motor boat there, for
fishing trips etc. so we were well done by.*

We felt particularly fortunate, for Jiff and Alan were already used to
this sort of trip, both of them at home in the bush and in the water in a
way Mark and I were not. They taught us to fish from the boat, to spot
game and I, always wary of water, even learned to snorkel, although the
water was not very clear. We had taken a stock of tins of food, but ate fresh
fish and decided, as Alan had a permit to shoot an animal strictly for our
own consumption, to go in search of game for the pot. This involved
leaving the game reserve early on Sunday for a nearby 'first class controlled
area'.

At 5 a.m., leaving Paul with Uelo, and baby Philip with the Bowmakers'
Henry, we piled Jeanne (now 2) and baby Caroline, plus carrycot, into the
cab of Alan's fisheries Land Rover, and with two Fisheries staff crouching
in the open back we bumped through trackless bush of a game reserve
area. We spotted a herd of elephant, hartebeest, ugly old warthogs,
bushbuck and dainty duiker, all relatively unafraid. Heading out of the
reserve itself we reached our destination – Lake Tondwa. Alan cut the
Land Rover's engine, we unfolded our sweaty limbs from the cab, placed
the sleeping baby in her carrycot in the shade of a thorn tree, and took in
the scene.

Everything was vast – the lake shimmering in the early sunlight, the
high, distant blue ridge of mountains behind it and above all, the silence.
It was as if the whole world had fallen still, leaving a silence deep enough
to drown in.

We broke it, of course, as humankind always does sooner or later. We
filed quietly through scrubby thorn bushes, spotted buck grazing, ears

flicking, alert. Alan selected a reedbuck in his sights. The heavy rifle's shot rang out like an explosion, sending terrified game into the bush and thousands of waterfowl up from the lake in panicked flocks. The buck was quickly skinned and gutted by the fisheries staff, its heart and liver a delicacy for them grilled over the breakfast fire. Back at Sumbu, its meat made delicious eating, as did two knob-nosed geese which Mark miraculously brought down with a single shot. As I wrote to my parents, with the game and waterfowl so relatively unafraid, this could not be regarded as sport, adding: *the tsetse flies were murder, and the mozzies, but it was extremely beautiful. We went for a couple of picnics on a lovely beach, under the shade of winter thorn trees which are elephants' favourite food, and mounds of dung warned us to keep a look-out! We saw several from the boat while fishing, also hippo, crocs and buck. With the water not clear, the fishing wasn't at its best, but we trawled around the coast a bit, with quite large plugs, and all caught about 3 to 4lbs nile perch. On the last day Mark thought he had hooked the bottom and reeled in a 17lbs perch! But frankly they aren't much sport as they hardly fight at all.*

***

My mention of the 'mozzies' and of sleeping nets down at lake level reminds me of a recent (2009) TV documentary, 'Guns, Germs and Steel', which showed the ravages wrought by malaria today. The example given was Zambia, showing the children's ward of Lusaka's main hospital, full of babies and children lying listless and clearly desperately ill. The presenter's doctor guide explains how malaria is ravaging the population, especially the young, now concentrated overwhelmingly in crowded urban areas. Yet I don't recall our worrying about the risk. Perhaps those whose work took them to lower altitudes and steamier heat were more likely to get it, for occasionally one heard of someone who had 'had a bad go' of it. We certainly took no prophylactics. Yet today malaria is one of the great scourges of tropical and sub-tropical Africa. Indeed 90% of malaria-related deaths are in sub-Saharan Africa, the majority of them among children under 5 years old. The parasites have become increasingly resistant to the main drugs used, and HIV infection increases individuals' susceptibility.

However, there is good news too: in April 2009 the United Nations news service announced that Zambia had joined several other African countries in slashing the number of deaths from malaria by more than half, through aggressive control measures. Between 2006 and 2008, 3.6 million long-lasting insecticidal [bed] nets were handed out, coinciding with a 47% decline in malaria deaths in the same period. The prevalence in parasites dropped too by 53%, and the percentage of children with severe anaemia – mostly caused by malaria – fell by 68%.

'Zambia stands as an example of what we can achieve throughout Africa through the combination of universal access to bed nets and effective malaria medicines', said the World Health Organisation.

***

It was now October, our 'pigeon pair' developing fast, Paul stringing words together at last ('lookadat!' was a first), Caroline over the worst of her digestive problems. I delighted in their difference: Paul so sturdy, strong and a real boy, Caroline small-boned and delicate, yet wiry and full of energy. She was variously described in letters to her grandparents as 'having a fearful temper but with a naughty sense of humour' (me) and 'a menace' (her doting father). This last was for her habit of waking the household at 5.30 a.m. and, at 8½ months, of spurning crawling in favour of standing upright like everyone else. This involved steadying herself determinedly on the furniture or, preferably, on Mum's legs, plus a great deal of falling over. She and Paul were good mates now, to my great delight, giggling together over toys, in the bath and side by side in two high chairs in the kitchen, where they swapped finger food and Paul ate heartily, his sister little. We took the plunge and put her into Paul's bedroom, where he was quite prepared to entertain her for an hour till we got up. The pleasure of remembering these scenes reminds me of how

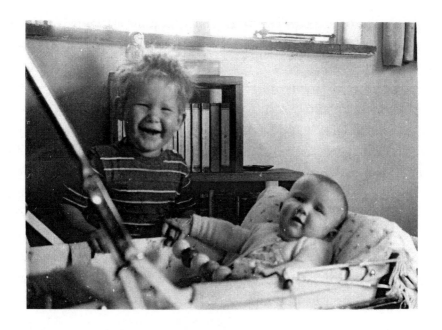

Our pigeon pair

...and feeling hot down at Mpulungu

hard it must have been for their grandparents, with only my letters and occasional tiny photos to keep them going. Already, though, I was writing home about the possibilities for our long leave the following year, and how we were saving for the airfares home.

Soon, in the final run-up to Independence, came another ball, and so another cabaret: this time to welcome visiting golfers for the Abercorn Open weekend, in which Mark, the club committee's golf member, was much involved. The theme was 'Caribbean' (sort of), the cabaret a series of musical(ish) numbers. Somewhere in the planning stage, when talents were being trawled from reluctant members, I admitted to playing the clarinet, which had lain untouched in a trunk since I had left home nearly five years before. Suddenly I was committed to playing in a small group, bizarrely named the Chila Chits, with Gavin Barr on guitar, Nobby Clark on banjo and Alan on tea chest bass. My repertoire was strictly classical, my comfort zone Bach rather than Bacharach, a sonatina sooner than swing, all played from sheet music. Now I must pick out a tune and play it from memory, with the gallant support and encouragement of the 'string section'. I recall wishing that I could 'swing it', improvise, jazz it up, and finding that it was just out of my reach. I could however play in tune with a decent tone, (much to Mark's astonishment, for it turned out that he had never heard me play). After much practising, I could manage 'Moon River', 'String of Pearls' and 'The Girl from Ipanema', moving on to include 'In the Mood', 'Bye Bye Blues' and we reached a triumphant climax with 'When the Saints Come Marching In'. The week before the ball, I wrote home with studied understatement of having too much to do: *The Ball is on Saturday, Ian Mackinson is giving drinks before it and I am making food for him,* [Barbara had gone ahead to UK] *and we are rehearsing nightly for the cabaret. On Sunday I am helping to do a buffet lunch for 50 at the club, making fruit flans, ham and several salads. The Open golf is over Sat. and Sun. and we are also having Jo Martin from Kasama for the w/e, a nice girl and the only eligible one for miles, so she'll be popular! I am trying to knock up a tropical dress, a one-shoulder drape in native cloth, and a cummerbund for Mark. – Now Mark has just been in with 2 VIP's from*

Salisbury he is entertaining, for coffee, and has now rushed to Kasama for the day with them, then Colin Carlin appeared for coffee and discussion on the dance – no wonder I never get everything done! Later I am going to Jiff to rig up dresses.

As *Abercornucopia* reported, on the night the Chila Chits, introduced by Ian our MC, were proclaimed a hit, as were ballads sung by Kevin Gould and Joan Carlin, Gavin's golf calypso and various mime-to-recordings numbers. Jo had brought with her another single girl, from V.S.O.: *the two girls had a terrific time with about ten bachelors between them. We danced madly till 1.30 a.m. and then to bed exhausted. Ian taped all the music which was v. good. On Sun. p.m. after working all morning on the buffet, I had super sailing while the golfers golfed. Won a thrilling race after a nasty pile-up at No. 3 Buoy where the leading boat capsized in a gale and we came up behind – as we went about my crew was warding off masts and booms with both hands! I then presented the golf prizes, having got the tinies to bed in the car early, and Mark made a v. good speech, but by 9.30 I was expiring of exhaustion.*

I never got to hear the tape recording Ian made of our group, to take to my parents when he returned to England, and perhaps it is just as well it has long since been lost.

Ode to My Merry Widow

Everybody had one – we believed
in its magic, the way it pushed
our breasts to pin-up proportions, and down
the front, over the fierce metal zip, the tiny
hooks and eyes we linked and linked
till voilà! – a neat wasp waist above
the swing of frilled suspenders.

My black lace merry widow,
where are you now? Is some young body
still prepared to bear the pinch and prod
of your wires and metal fixings? More likely
you went to landfill, lacy nylon dissolving
amidst cans and cartons, your metal ribs
still lying, skeletal, in the sand.

CHAPTER 12

Flags exchanged at midnight: of dreaded farewells and a longed-for arrival

People are getting rather apprehensive about Independence, I wrote in mid-October 1964, *though I don't feel they'll really bother to make trouble.* It was, both Mark and I felt, all somewhat of a formality, but for those settlers who had lived in the country for decades, perhaps their whole lives, it was much harder to come to terms with. And for the careers of those Britons who had worked for the Northern Rhodesia Government, there were step changes ahead, if not already faced. Nonetheless, the Union flag would be coming down for the last time: *We want to go to the flag lowering and raising etc. in the township at midnight on 23rd, but not if it means standing pressed in a sweaty throng. Pam [our neighbour] may baby-sit for us, we can't take children in the car down there.*

Abercornucopia published a full centre page spread of the forthcoming independence weekend celebrations programme. It would begin during Friday with 'arrival of people from rural areas', then an evening torchlight procession through the township to the Independence Ground was to be followed by 'traditional dances and songs, a parade of Messengers, Kapasus,

Youth league and prayers for the new nation', before the midnight flag lowering and raising ceremony. Saturday would start with prayers and services at St Francis Mission and the church, a gathering with the Tanganyika Brass Band would be followed by the reading of the new president's message, the firing of rockets and a flypast of Red Locust Control aircraft dropping Zambian flags. Then a parade, cycle races, football matches, a cocktail party at the District Secretary's residence ('by invitation'), a cinema show and open air concert and dancing from 9 p.m. Sunday would be quieter: more services of worship followed by inter-schools sports and football, closing with ballroom dancing at the Catholic Welfare Hall and traditional dancing at Independence Ground.

While all this was going on, Abercorn would also be making a unique contribution to the national celebrations, as our newspaper headlined. Following a precedent set by Kenya and neighbouring Tanganyika and Malawi, the new flag was to be raised at midnight on the country's highest (6,782 ft) peak, Mount Sunzu, 21 miles away by road and close to the border with Tanganyika. This 'strenuous expedition', *Abercornucopia* reported, would be undertaken by the training staff at Abercorn's Outward Bound School, adding: 'A fine view of the table-like summit about 17 miles away is gained from Abercorn airport, and it can be seen from many villages in the surrounding countryside; but in general the country is thinly populated by not very advanced people who will probably be somewhat puzzled by this unusual light high on their night-time horizon.'

In the run-up to the weekend I wrote home: *The town is decked in Zambian flags (so ugly – black, red, green, orange) processions rehearsing etc. Jiff and Alan are coming to supper and bridge on Friday and we all go to Independence Ground at 10.30 p.m. or so. There is a Tanganyika brass band, and fortunately places in an enclosure for 2/- to avoid being trampled! ... As we have to give the servants most of the w/e off we shall be busy watering flowers and veg. We haven't any fixtures at the Club – some people are fearfully anti and won't go to the ceremony or anything, but it seems silly as the Union Jack only represents what went a while ago now.*

In the event, though, I found the moment more moving than I had expected. After tribal dancing (*so feeble, just jigging about, no costumes and endless microphone commentary*), and a 50-strong brass band from Tanganyika R.C Mission (*splendid*), I suddenly felt a wave of sadness as we watched the old Union flag's jerky descent: *I thought of all the pioneers who'd worked under it, but the mob cheered, and the other flag went up – v. ugly really. The anthem however is really beautiful, 'Nkosi Sikelele Africa' originally, and the Chila Chits have played it for you not v. well on the vast tape Ian is bringing over for you.* (The anthem, or at least its tune, is now much more widely known, having become the national anthem for the new, democratic South Africa in the 1990's. I still find it both beautiful and moving).

We were part of the 250-strong official cocktail party on the Saturday at the Barrs', racially mixed of course, although this was still a novelty for many in the European community. For the first time we met some of the local officials and functionaries of the new administration. I remember my continuing feelings of awkwardness as I tried to make conversation with them, though I described the party to my parents only as 'good for a laff'.

There were other signs of changing times: our local M.P. was to be posted to Moscow, to join Zambia's new embassy there. It was rumoured that he had married a second wife to take with him. (Ian Mackinson in his autobiography writes of a common practice at this time of taking an additional 'cocktail' wife, a younger woman readier to adapt to the demands of western culture, often to the relief of the first, traditionally home-based wife.) 'Vesey' – Desmond Vesey-Fitzgerald, our own world-renowned naturalist, announced he would be leaving, appointed as Scientific Officer to Tanganyika's National Parks department – the start of Abercorn's own brain-drain, as the newspaper had it. And there were more farewell parties, including for Paddy and Glenda Tobin – both mainstays of the club, she a fellow bunny girl and sailor – who were off to Mongu.

We looked, I think, for signs of things going wrong, confirmation of predictions that standards would deteriorate. No letter from Mum this week meant 'posts slowing down I suppose'. The 500 miles of phone lines that linked Abercorn to the Copper Belt were down again – 'it's due to a shortage of technicians'. Mark had his watch and wallet (both gifts from me) together with the hefty sum of £30, stolen from his bedside in Mpika, a costly loss for us and with little hope of anything being found, for 'the police in Mpika were very inefficient'. Mark was away a lot now: *I am having a thoroughly boring week as he is away Mon. – Fri. and the line to Kasama is out of order so I can't even hear from him. I for one am getting thoroughly sick of this job – if he isn't away it's a Liemba weekend or the phone never stops from 7 a.m. or we have to entertain company trogs. No word of his leave yet either. Shirley Macdonald says it is impossible to rent a house in Lusaka, so what we shall do I don't know.*

As I recall those months after independence and reread my letters – a mix, by now, of aerogrammes scrawled 'in haste', of sheets off an airmail pad at Christmas time and, for one later momentous announcement, two close-typed quarto pages – they bring me what I can only describe as a feel of autumn: of the tail end of a long, sunny summer, of falling leaves reminding us of colder months to come; of packing away the sun umbrella, unwrapping packages of papery bulbs to plant for spring. Fanciful perhaps, but it is the only way I can describe the different feel this period gives me now. It was a time full of uncertainties and conflicting emotions, for we now knew we would be leaving by March the following year and that, wherever we fetched up, it could not compare with Abercorn and the wonderful little community we had become a part of. At least, I thought, Mark's next posting was into sales, a promotion away from the field. I and the children would see more of him, even though my memories of Lusaka were not positive. I was gearing myself too for our long leave: the plan was for me to fly to England with the children upon our departure from Abercorn, Mark joining us at my parents' once he had settled into Lusaka.

So my letters now were full of excitement about seeing them all, but also of practical considerations. There were anticipatory wails about the cold of an English winter, of needing little vests, requests for jumpers to be knitted please, of how I was making Paul long corduroy trousers for Christmas and how Caroline could nearly walk but would have no shoes. Soon I was imagining us actually staying there, of spending time with the family: my clarinet now oiled and used again, I was pulling from my music case piano and clarinet arrangements, pieces Mum and I could play together. Ian Mac promised to take the piano parts to her, along with the tape of the band's music making. I remember wondering what the new family home, a restored old vicarage in a Cambridgeshire village, would be like, for I had only a couple of small 'before and after' snaps of the outside to go on. I hoped, I wrote, that the children's room would not be too close to their grandparents', with their habit of waking at dawn, and with Caroline sure to be teething again.

But I am – as I was then – getting ahead of myself. With life beginning to feel less secure, less certain, I am not surprised now to read – though I have no specific memory of it – that by December my back was '*agony*', so much so that I was lying down and resting whenever I could. Which can't have been very often, with Mark away on business, or at weekends on Liemba duty, or with the golf team for a match; with my music practice for the band's next appearance and a looming Club AGM for which I, as retiring hon. sec., must produce agendas for 100 members. By the time we had the Yacht Club's barbecue, the rains had started in earnest and we had to move the cooking into the boat house – '*it will smell of mutton for months*', I wrote. But the rain cleared, and the band played our now familiar favourites as we gathered on the balcony lit with fairy lights. It was a beautiful spot, that balcony, with on a quieter night just the slip-slop sound of little waves and the surrounding darkness – that proper darkness which has vanished now from so much of the inhabited world, a darkness in which, when the clouds cleared, you could see a dazzle of stars.

By mid-December Christmas had been on my mind for weeks, what with the ordering and posting of cards and gifts for the overseas post. We were proud of our card that year – a fine sketch of the Yacht Club's boat house by Ian Mac, which had also appeared on the front page of the independence issue of *Abercornucopia*. Now we were planning a shared festive feast with the Bowmakers, and had the luxury of Mark being grounded for a month, covering duties at the Abercorn depot while his clerk was on leave. No nights away, no worrying about him driving on roads made more dangerous by the rains. We were enjoying this new routine when we were knocked sideways by a totally unexpected development.

Mark came home one lunch time white faced, holding a terse note from the Zambia Manager in Lusaka, saying Mark would now not be going to sales, but as a rep. again, to Broken Hill (a small town on the Copper Belt). This was very clearly a demotion, the sales patch smaller even than Mark's previous one in Gwelo, but the note contained no explanation. Mark was devastated; after a miserable weekend agonising over it, he decided to telegram for permission to fly down to Lusaka and find out what was really going on.

He did not get much joy: the manager was a tough-talking Australian with no gift for managing people (it was rumoured he had admitted he would not be long in Zambia due to poor staff relations). Face to face, he used words like 'mediocre' and 'apathetic', justifying a 'lateral transfer', whilst admitting that Mark's customer relations and PR were 'excellent'. Mark talked to colleagues too, one of whom had had similar treatment and had stuck it out. Mark came home angry, frustrated and depressed.

It is always hard being the powerless spouse having to stand by and watch the hurt. My reaction was an intense sense of loyalty and of fury on his behalf. I hammered out my anger and anxiety on the depot's typewriter in a long letter to both sets of parents, timed not to reach them until after Christmas:

It makes me so angry, when I think of the amount of work Mark has done since he has been here, and how the company comes before everything with him, the weekends he works, the long hours etc. It is me who moans and groans, while he throws himself right into it, and gets this for it. It is a great blow to hear of the sort of appreciation they have for all his work and loyalty. Excuse my getting heated... all the good men in the Zambia company are leaving, by resignation if they can't get a transfer away...

To make matters worse for Mark, the overall General Manager, based in Salisbury, was on long leave, his stand-in *'an old nit waiting for retirement.'* And although my letter does not mention it, I kept remembering how this self-same manager and his wife had been good friends in the early Salisbury days, even being special guests at my 21st birthday dinner five years before. But that seemed an age ago now, and already we were beginning to think our way out of the situation:

The thing is to decide if there is a future on this basis for Mark. We think not, but of course I just have to tell him that I will support what he decides, and it's no good drudging along with no heart in it for people who obviously don't like you, which is what he says it is, when one could make a fresh start, even though with some worry and loss financially to start with. He hasn't actually said he will leave, but inferred it. We think we are on 3 months notice, in which we would include our next year's leave if possible, so needn't do anything till about February… I realise that what with Will thinking of going into the Church, and Simon madly in love, and James waiting to see if he's got to Oxford, this must be just about too much to take! There is nothing definite, except our depression and disappointment – and all the while we thought Mark was off to Lusaka for a super promotion. Ha ha.

Paul can't believe his luck…

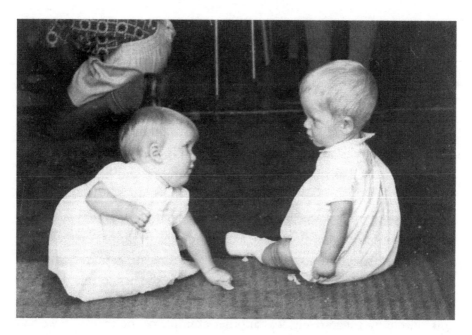

...while Caroline (left) prefers sharing soggy biscuit with Philip Bowmaker

I knew it would be a great worry for both sets of parents. In addition, Mark's father had been a big wheel in the company in South Africa, and must have known some of those involved and wondered what to advise, aware there were no strings he could pull.

By a horrible coincidence, the Bowmakers were also dealing with the implications of a career set-back for Alan in the Fisheries Department. Plans for him to go to headquarters in Lusaka had been abruptly cancelled, and they were having to adapt to staying on till their long leave, and were talking of his finding another job, perhaps in South Africa. My letter ended with more general news: due to a rabies outbreak in the African township, all loose dogs would be shot, so our Alsatian Boy was ignominiously tied to the garage after a week of fun with his 'girlfriend' on heat. The Nativity Play was that evening, I was making scores of orange jellies for the children's Christmas party next day. The last refrigerated truck of fresh goods before Christmas had arrived, and someone had fallen off a ladder while decorating the club hall and had to have 11 stitches.

Posts were very slow and the Christmas cake from home had not arrived. Queues outside the bank had been so long, as people waited to change their hoarded cash for the new Zambian note, that twice someone had fainted in the heat. The rains were exceptionally heavy.

There was nothing for it but to throw ourselves into the Christmas celebrations, not least for the children, for it would be the first when Paul would really appreciate what it was all about. His eyes were wide as Father Christmas arrived at the club party on a fire engine and handed a gift to each child.

We hid a goodly stack of parcels from England until the day itself. On Christmas morning the Bowmakers came round with gifts – toys for the children, and a godmother present for Caroline of a pottery Samuel Whiskers, the start of a Beatrix Potter set which she has to this day. Jiff's gift for Mark, a shaped drawstring bag in flesh pink crepe, in which two golf balls hung suggestively, was another example of the creativity we had to bring to bear, given the limitations of what was available. Caroline slept through the hearty carols in church, then it was on to the Barrs and the Vermeulens for drinks, neighbours Robin and Pam to drinks with us and bachelor Colin to lunch. To make room for evening dinner we swam, then shared an evening feast at the Bowmakers followed by roulette. The sun lasted for our midday Pimms party on Boxing Day, which I enjoyed despite an increasingly sore toe, which I had stubbed down at the Yacht Club on Christmas Eve. More fun for the children that afternoon was our first visit to the nuns, being made a fuss of by Sisters Amabilis and Romana with little cakes and crackers, and a tour round their house and little chapel. And who could forget the all-male panto at the evening club hop, with the thunder of heavy dancing feet, falsetto dialogue and a huge fairy queen with 'the hairiest legs of any fairy ever to grace a stage'? For the club's New Year's Eve dance cabaret, Gavin and I prepared a special arrangement of 'Stranger on the Shore', one of Britain's top hits of 1962.

There remains one mystery from that Christmas: I wrote to thank my mother for *the grey wig, which is rather a nice one*. A *grey* wig? Not for me, surely? Could it have been for a wicked stepmother in that panto? The question hangs spectrally in the air, unanswerable now.

From Mark to my parents, early January 1965: *No doubt Amanda has told you all about our Christmas and New Year's doings... all very pleasant. Unfortunately the poor girl stubbed her toe at the yacht club on Christmas Eve. The doctor looked at it at our Pimms party on Boxing Day and declared it a mere bruise. However, a week later it was still causing considerable pain and preventing sleep so she went back to him. Now he has decided it is more serious and put it in plaster... unfortunately (typical of this country I'm afraid) the X-ray machine is broken so we don't know for certain what's wrong. Poor Amanda is rather crippled...*

As you will have gathered we are getting rather fed up with this country and with the company here... I feel I may as well get out, what to do I don't know... anyway we shall be coming over soon, looking forward to seeing you and showing off the grandchildren... All a rather disturbing start to 1965 but I hope the year will end well. Please pray for us.

'Poor Amanda' – but also poor Mark, who was now both depot clerk and chief homemaker, bathing children, getting up to Paul with his bad cold in the night, cooking suppers. To cap it all the depot safe was burgled, and Caroline had caught a mild form of chickenpox, with Paul sure to be next. At least Mark was grounded and so not expected to be covering his territory till the clerk returned. We were now spending much time talking about the future: the company's personnel department was urging Mark to wait for the General Manager's return, felt there would be a future for him. But Mark was becoming increasingly certain that the sort of job he had been doing was not for him. Somewhere we had heard of psychological aptitude testing, and I wrote to Mum asking her to find out more. And where should we settle? We didn't feel we wanted to return to Zambia – *Abercorn is the only really nice place, and its all getting more inefficient and maddening daily* I wrote. So that left Britain or South Africa. I had deep, though unarticulated misgivings about the latter, with apartheid dominating all aspects of life there, whilst Mark, who had never lived in England apart from his three years at Cambridge University, felt he belonged in Africa. I knew that my role was to support my husband who was, after all, the breadwinner. Meanwhile though, *do we sell everything here before we go, or hang on and have to come back (Mark will be in Broken Hill for the 6 weeks before he comes over), and so on. All v. difficult, but I'm sure it will work out and Mark will find what really suits him.*

I can see now, through our letters, how much more of a burden our situation must have been for Mark than for me. I, in my role as follower, as loyal wife, found that by not thinking about the future too deeply, I could stay optimistic, with a naïve confidence in his future career. Besides, I was soon to be going home, and my letters are full of practicalities about push chairs, cots and possible toys for the grandchildren. I was going home to a place where, even in a house I had never seen, everything else would be familiar. Each piece of well-worn old furniture, every picture and wall mirror, every table setting – the faded pretty china, the twirly silver candlesticks, the napkin rings we had each had since we were little – all would be just as I had always known it. The grandfather clock would tick and whir, Mum's dented saucepans would clatter in the kitchen, her clutter of letters, bills and messages on scraps of paper lie in drifts by the phone. There would be croquet on the lawn, beyond it Pa's apple trees, and surely an asparagus bed, a fruit cage and tall globe artichokes. My Gran – Mum's mother – had just moved into a little house across the road; there I would find her, her Chinese carpet in the drawing room, the chiming carriage clock on the mantelpiece, her Steinway grand piano with its double piano stool for duets, a faint smell of pot pourri and her lively voice: 'Darling! How wonderful to see you!'. I had all this to come, to show my children and make them part of. Whilst Mark, sole breadwinner, would be stuck with working out his two months' notice in Broken Hill, certain only of what he did not want to do for a living.

By the end of January we had decided: Cape Town it would be, a choice welcomed by both our parents. *And a big thing is the better communications with you, and mail ships not so expensive as planes to Zambia.* With an unaffordable quote for moving all our furniture, I set about turning out cupboards, and suddenly we were the ones having sales of small items, flagging up larger ones for later offers. Almost nothing need be thrown

Lake Tanganyika regatta: M.V. Triton and dinghies

away, for any battered utensil or torn sheet would fetch a few pennies. The fridge found a new home in Fort Rosebery, our double bed a new lease of life in an African's home in the township. In the end we kept little but our chintz-covered suite and small tables. Even the dining room table and chairs in some dark hardwood, that Mark had stripped and polished so lovingly, were up for sale. But my desk, an antique but solid oak bureau given to me by Gran, at which I had written so many letters home, would go with us no matter what it cost. (Today, refurbished, it stands in Caroline's home, its pigeon holes and little drawers cleared out, looking better than ever.)

At about the same time there was a cheering treat: the Yacht Club executed a long discussed plan for a regatta on Lake Tanganyika. Somehow all the dinghies were transported down in advance, trailers bouncing down the 28 miles of dirt road. We left home early for what turned into an unforgettable day. There were spectators both on the overlooking cliff-top and on the shore, with such interest in the event that Ann Parton and her helpers prepared lunch for 60 Abercornians. At that lower altitude the heat was tremendous, and a paddling area was set up in the shade for the children. How different from little Lake Chila! We were to sail off Niamukolo Point, with Peter Parton's M.V. Triton as committee boat some 200 yards off shore. Those vast expanses of water (I still had a niggle of anxiety at the immense depths below us) and a fine wind at the start made for superb sailing, then the wind dropped and races, now much slower, had to be rationed, each sailor having a turn at two long races. Lighter winds gave me a bit of an advantage, and I proudly wrote home that I had *tied equal first in one with Colin and another chap!* which made an excellent excuse to leave the boats down there for a tie-breaker the following weekend. To end the day, William Winterton, about to return to England after his year's voluntary service, hosted a barbecue at his caravan, the centre piece a whole roast lamb on a spit. The follow-on day was just as good, with a rice salad lunch and 'plenty of time to improve our suntans', though Mark was busy supervising the Liemba's unloading into the fuel depot, and I finished only third overall.

February, then, was our last month in Abercorn. We had been married for four years now, celebrated by inviting the Bowmakers and Colin to dinner, suddenly nostalgic:
- Remember how cold it was, and how my veil was whipped up by the wind for the photos? I said
- A year later we were in Cape Town with Paul, and Dad cracked open a bottle of Krug, said Mark, adding: ...and two years ago we were still in Gwelo, waiting for your Ma to visit ...
- And last year I was enormous and fed up, and Caroline arrived two days later!
    Her first birthday was a low key affair, overshadowed as it was by packing and promises of buying her better toys in England. She was now able to walk, and quite apart from having to keep even more vigilant track of her, we had to deal with Paul's frustration as his newly assertive sister attempted to join his games or seize his toys. There were frequent incidents that ended in tears on both sides. Then, what with the children

Last trip on Lake Tanganyika: still 'the blonder the better'

and I getting tonsillitis, measles spreading in the township and a worsening rabies outbreak, it began to feel as though things were conspiring to make our last weeks difficult. *This place is a hotbed of disease,* I wrote dramatically, with *Mark overworked as mother's help.* Then the company joined the conspiracy, perversely ordering Mark to spend his last full working week at a sales conference in Broken Hill, thus cutting short our last weekend among our Abercorn friends before our departure on the following Friday.

Still, we had one last good day down at Lake Tanganyika: Mark's manager Peter Hare, brassed off with his own impending demotion to Salisbury, drove up for a last trip on the company. We borrowed Alan's fisheries launch for the morning, and despite storms circling around, managed to get to the Kalambo Falls for a last look at the storks floating above the spray.

Mark's replacement, Dick Hurlbatt, had already been up for two days to look around: *He is probably going to have our house, they are keen gardeners, he seems quite nice. He's full of enthusiasm for the job – poor soul,* I added darkly. He would have two weeks overlap with Mark, so the first would be spent largely away from Abercorn. I began to plan introducing him and his wife Jane around – until they arrived, one of their children with full-blown measles. Feeling guiltily inhospitable, we had no alternative but to avoid them.

Abercorn had one last social event in store for us: I had been involved in organising, in the new post-independence spirit, a multi-racial fund-raising dance in aid of a university for Zambia. We decided on the TVMI as venue, being neutral territory, not exclusively associated, as the club was, with the white population. Tickets were sold as widely as possible and many of us whites went in support of this good cause, together with numerous smartly dressed local Africans. There was however one problem, for none of them had brought their wives, and the resulting shortage of female dance partners meant an exhausting but also laughter filled evening for us women who were there. No sooner had one sat down to mop one's face and rest aching feet after gamely twisting to Chubby Checker, than another smiling black face would appear, and one was swept off to rock 'n roll to 'Love Me Do'.

My memories of our last days in Abercorn, apart from that evening and our breathless laughter, are at best hazy, blurred I think now by the mix of emotions I was having to deal with. I know, only because my letters tell me, that my last club AGM went off well, and I expect I was warmly thanked for all my hard work. We invited 12 to meet the Hurlbatts, who presumably had found a baby sitter for their children (the second one now having caught the measles), and it apparently went off fine. There was, I wrote, one last sailing regatta on little Lake Chila, at which I tied first with Alan, my long-held ambition to beat him finally thwarted. And I am touched now to read, in an issue of *Abercornucopia* that must have come out just before our departure, a warm send-off piece John Carlin had written about Mark's and my contribution to Abercorn life, even referring to me as 'Abercornucopia's dear Amanda'. Dear John – I realise now how very fond I was of him too.

The Barrs, bless them, kindly invited us to stay for the last three nights in their official residence's guest house in the grounds, as all but our suitcases had gone on the removers' van or to local buyers, from whom we had made the fine sum of £150 'to put aside for our next home'. We were, I wrote home, invited out every night of our final week, and each evening must have been a reminder of how many good friends we had made and the unspoken fear that we might never meet again, for who knew where we might all end up living?

As I wrote my last letter home, my thoughts were clearly darting ahead, back to present practicalities, then ahead once more: *I think I just about have a warm outfit for each to arrive in. I must say I dread leaving here by plane, everyone coming to the airport to wave, and feeling one won't see little Abercorn ever again. See you SOON! I can't wait – but am depressed at leaving poor Mark for 6 weeks... so many goodbyes to be said ......*

However, said they had to be, with many a last hug amongst a throng of well-wishers on the tarmac at the little airfield. From an early age I had learned not to cry, and boarding school from the age of nine had given me plenty of practice. But now, strapped into our seats in the little plane as it rose from the airfield, I peered through the window at the tiny figures waving and waving, the image blurring with my tears. Then we were into cloud, and the captain was, as usual, warning of turbulence. Hastily I wiped my eyes and turned to attend to the children.

In Lusaka there was a last link with Southern Rhodesia, for it now held our friends John and Shirley Macdonald, last seen in Bulawayo expecting their much longed-for baby. Their Hilary and our two played as Mark and I geared ourselves for the following day's flight, the VC10 that would take me and our children to London's Heathrow Airport, via an evening refuelling stopover in Nairobi. It was another departure I dreaded, this time with a longed-for arrival at its end.

'We've made it,' I thought, as I heard the VC10's engines change their note, then the pilot's announcement. The children had enjoyed bustling Nairobi airport, and had slept thereafter. Somehow we were now changed into our skeleton winter wardrobe, Caroline, who had only ever worn cotton tops and a nappy, a sleeveless frock for best, very puzzled by leggings, but shoeless. Paul, who usually went barefoot, at least had a pair of wide Bata sandals, with warm corduroys and his only sweater.

I remember clearly how, as we stood at the top of the long flight of steps from the plane, the freezing night air caught in my lungs. It was four a.m., the airport bright with lights and bustle in the darkness. And after we had queued through passport control and customs, after I had found all our luggage and loaded it onto a trolley, after I had settled Caroline into the little hand luggage basket and shown Paul how to help me push the trolley through the last barrier, there, all lined up waving and smiling, was my family. Heaven knows what time they must have got up, to be there to meet us, but here were the dear familiar faces of my Ma and Pa, and of my three brothers Will, Simon and James.

In my parents' new cream Rover I watched the dawn come slowly, first over suburban rows of little brick houses, the roads so neatly edged with kerbstones, and then over an unfamiliar more rural landscape as we left the sprawls of London behind, heading north towards their new Cambridgeshire home. A weak sun appeared, low in a pale sky, as the small neat fields sped past, hedgerows and winter stubble rimed with frost, a church spire appearing among the skeletons of bare trees. Paul stirred and woke, looked sleepily around. 'Look, Paul,' I said, pointing out of the window, 'this is England.' 'England' he repeated experimentally.

At some deep level I recognised the four years that had passed for what they were – vivid years full of growing up and learning, of building a family and making friends, all in the bright, hot sunshine of colonial Africa. As the little plane had risen above Abercorn, I had already sensed that it was a life that could never be recreated elsewhere. But young Amanda was not one for looking back; now I and my two beautiful children were home, where a part of me would always belong, and that for the moment was enough.

POSTSCRIPT

It has been a long journey, this travelling back to such a distinctive period in my life. The writing process has often been an exploration, part archaeology – bringing up to the light old memories, documents, photos – part further education to overcome my own ignorance, part my attempts at interpretation in the light of all of these.

I had remained over the intervening years largely ignorant of both countries' earlier histories and cultures and of how these could explain much of what came after. So the journey has involved a lot of reading, from history to novels to web explorations on Wikipedia and its links to other sources. It has also required many a 'dig' through layers of memory, often frustrated at its quixotic unreliability. I discovered that, while I could be prompted to recall much more than I had expected, there were also strange 'black holes'; a face, a name, a voice had inexplicably migrated to some inaccessible part of my brain. Yet other memories – a particular moment, a scene, even an emotional state – are indelibly etched and can be summoned at will. Sometimes my interpretation of what I was working on could change, much like the shifting patterns we see through a kaleidoscope. A quick shake – in my case a session of dead-heading in the garden, a solitary walk, a night's sleep – and presto! a pattern could be transformed, if I was lucky, an insight gained.

Parts of the journey have been hard, the road stony. The appearance of my brother Simon's letters home from Gwelo, an 18-year old's account of our life, forced me to think much harder about my young self, and in particular her attitudes and behaviour to black people. Indeed, early on I thought of the writer of my letters as 'her', as a different person whom I could observe and write about, but not as my self. After all, I reasoned, I have changed so much over 40 plus years, and it is true that there is much of young Amanda's attitudes and behaviours that I am happy to have left behind. But as we have journeyed together over these years of writing and of exploration, I have come to accept that she is part of me.

Writing my way through those four Rhodesia years, I have also found myself thinking more and more of the people whose lives touched ours, often in significant ways, sad at how we had lost touch with so many. My only constant link to that time has been Jiff and Alan Bowmaker, Jiff and I steadfast correspondents, godmothers to each others' youngest, graduating over the decades from air letters to audio tapes to emails. They left Abercorn later the same year as us, for Salisbury, Alan ultimately to the university there, and where their second son, James, was born. The family fetched up in South Africa where Alan ran Durban's Sea World, retired to a farm near Pietermaritzburg where they and son Philip raise day-old chicks.

But where are others we knew at that time? At my PC, checking for news of Zimbabwe whilst following the tortuous negotiations between President Robert Mugabe's ZANU/PF and challenger Morgan Tsvangirai's MDC, I found myself registering on a website for those nostalgic for the old days of Rhodesia / Zimbabwe. There I scanned lists of names from our old suburb in Gwelo/Gweru, to no avail so far. I had long ago heard that Jack and Joy Crouch, who were so supportive of me as a young mum in Gwelo, had headed for Canada. John and Shirley Macdonald went, I think, to Hong Kong. As my focus headed north to Abercorn, I discovered a website for old Northern Rhodesians and there I registered again, found so many people doing the same, searching for old school mates, work colleagues, even one for his father, with a sad 'we lost touch'.

One early stroke of luck was news of the existence of the Northern Rhodesian Pensioners Association, through whose kind offices my letters reached four old friends. Gavin and Caroline Barr, whom we saw so much of in Abercorn, are now happily living in Kent after a career that had taken them to various parts of the world. Ian and Barbara Mackinson, last heard of visiting my parents on Boxing Day 1964, are living in Hampshire not far from many of their family. Ian had returned to Zambia after independence to help build its new civil service, and his memoir, *Footsteps in the Dust*, has been invaluable in teaching me more about the British administration of Northern Rhodesia, his career for 15 years until independence. Facebook at last yielded up a connection with Colin Carlin, living with a large family in Bath and enjoying many a 'When we ... ' reminiscence of Abercorn days with his own network. Through him I learned that his parents John and Sheelagh retired to South Africa's Garden Route in the late 1960's, then for health reasons moving to Cape Town. Sheelagh, after John's death there, moved to London to live happily with Colin and his new family. Another chance search with Google unexpectedly and delightfully put me in contact with Sisters Amabilis and Romana, now both living in adjacent convents in Uxbridge, U.K.

But what of Daniel and Inez, of Uelo and Friday, who polished our floors and ironed every garment, minded our children, dug and watered our gardens? I wonder now what might have happened to them? We can at best speculate, and for that we must look at what has happened to the countries they lived in. Daniel and Inez returned to Nyasaland as we left Gwelo, just before the country gained its independence as Malawi in 1964. Under Dr Hastings Banda (he of the homburg hat and little fly whisk) it became a one-party state, his dictatorial regime only ending 30 years later with the first multi-party elections. It is one of the poorest countries in the world, tiny (smaller than England), landlocked, with none of the mineral wealth of its near neighbours Zambia and the Congo, its jewel that other lake at the end of the Great Rift Valley, Lake Malawi, third largest in Africa. Agriculture is the main activity, tobacco its principal export, child tobacco pickers 'poisoned by nicotine' according to a recent report from international children's organisation Plan. Average life expectancy is around 50 years, poverty, AIDS and HIV having taken a dreadful toll on the health of the people. Given all that, Daniel and Inez, who would be in their 70's now, will be exceptionally old in their community if they are still alive. Still, that is how I like to think of them, senior citizens in their village, their children and grandchildren around them.

What, I wonder, if they had chosen to remain in Southern Rhodesia?

Under Ian Smith's Rhodesian Front, elected when we lived in Gwelo, things would have gone on the same for a while, as 'Smithy' pressed the British Government for independence. Frustrated, he signed the country's Unilateral Declaration of Independence (UDI) in 1965, and with the tacit support of South Africa settled down to survive international sanctions. (When I visited the Bowmakers in Salisbury briefly in 1970, I found a beleaguered but defiant white community, proud of its self-sufficiency amidst empty shop shelves and roads full of elderly cars.) Through the 1970's though, nationalist groups escalated guerrilla attacks into a full-scale 'Bush War' or 'Chimurenga', the traumatic effects of which were felt by everyone, black and white, country or city dweller. An estimated 20,000 people died. UDI failed however, not because of sanctions, but the ebbing away of support from Rhodesia's neighbours; by March 1980, after the London Agreement ceasefire, Robert Mugabe had been elected and the country became the independent state of Zimbabwe. (I have a family connection here: my father, then deputy director of the Joint Intelligence Bureau in London, had been tasked with advising Prime Minister Harold Wilson on the likely effectiveness of sanctions as a way of bringing down Smith's regime. He was unequivocal in his advice that it would fail. When it did and Wilson was challenged, he claimed that he was only following his civil servants' advice. Pa, relating this to me some time later, remained incandescent with rage at this dishonesty and never forgave Wilson.)

The Marxist Mugabe was, as Martin Meredith's 'State of Africa' makes clear, always committed to the creation of a one-party state, as well as being a believer in violence to achieve his ends. Zimbabwe under his increasingly despotic rule has slid tragically from being the 'bread basket of Southern Africa' to a broken country in need of aid of every kind, violence the currency of government. With the collapse of a previously effective health care system, average life expectancy has plummeted to a level similar to Malawi's, Aids and HIV gaining a grip among a people weakened by starvation. As I write this (in 2009) the attempt at power sharing with Morgan Tsvangirai's opposition Movement for Democratic

Change, elected in 2008 but blocked from taking power, has failed to convince the international community that a promised programme of aid should yet be implemented.

Up in Zambia, those two bright cheerful young men Uelo and Friday stayed on in Abercorn, though not I think to work for our successors. They would be a little younger than Daniel now, perhaps 60-something. Maybe they continued to live in the Mbala area, though if they were ambitious for wider opportunities they would have had to travel further afield, as the town became even more isolated from the rest of the country. Perhaps they went down to Mpulungu which has fared better, becoming, so Colin Carlin reports, 'a thriving trans-African trading centre, with merchants from across the continent flocking to buy and sell local produce, fish and almost everything else. The Liemba still steams down the lake, but has long since ceased to tow that oil barge down from Tanzania, supplies now coming in on Zambia's joint rail link with Tanzania, the TAZARA Railway, built in the 1970's by Chinese from north of Lusaka across to Dar es Salaam on the coast.

As for Abercorn – Mbala – it has been left isolated, with roads degraded, the Great North Road that used to pass Abercorn diverted now to the east, and the little airport taken over by the Zambian Air Force, all scheduled and private flights stopped. Recent photos show Lake Chila much as it was, though with no sign of any sailing dinghies, and according to Colin the Yacht Club is now a ZAF Officers' Mess. The Tanganyika Victoria Memorial Institute, the dear old TVMI, where once we went to the fortnightly film shows and which housed the little library, now 'makes a handsome Town Hall for the Mayor', writes Colin. Once a key outpost of early British colonial control, the town is a quiet backwater, its Greek and Indian traders and its expat. community long gone.

Sadly, this lack of transport has hindered the development of both agriculture and tourism in the area, despite all that it has to offer. As for the country, its first president Kenneth Kaunda, like his Malawi neighbour, soon recognised the attractions of a one-party state, and remained in power until he was ousted in 1991 in elections vigorously campaigned for by the Movement for Multi-party Democracy. By this time the mineral-rich country with its huge potential wealth had slipped to being one of the world's poorest. Average life expectancy is around 43 years, HIV/Aids the main cause of adult deaths.

And what of us, the little family that left the new Zambia in early 1965? We sailed as planned from Southampton for Cape Town on the MV Pendennis Castle for a new life, I with some misgivings, Mark armed with guidance pointing him in the direction of work in computer systems. '*I don't think we shall stay here long*', I wrote home in an early letter, '*as really politically it is most unsavoury and unchristian*'. But we did – I for seven years, Mark to this day, seeing in the new, democratic South Africa. Cape Town was and is a beautiful city and we led a good life – a life full of privileges reserved for white people. Ironically it was the injustices of apartheid that taught me to regard black Africans with greater respect, to see the good women who worked for us – first Victoria Nkosi, then, when she was 'endorsed out' to a remote so-called homeland in the Eastern Cape, Vivian Mpendukane – as individuals deserving of my consideration and regard, not least for the resourceful ways they coped under the weight of a system that constrained every aspect of their lives. I stood with other women members of the Black Sash outside Parliament and on street corners, in silent protest at the continued injustices (the sash representing mourning for the death of the constitution and the rule of law), ignoring my father-in-law's unspoken displeasure. But by 1970 Mark's and my marriage had foundered and we divorced. Needing work, I found it at the university's computer centre, where my boss – the 'Prof' – was Dennis Parkyn; and by 1972 he and I were living together, planning his year's academic sabbatical in England. Paul, Caroline and his son Geoff came with us to Bristol.

There we took the difficult decision to stay here, despite the consequences for our families and the separation from their father that it meant for my children. Life in the English Midlands, after a period of readjustment, has treated us well, Paul and Caroline receiving an excellent state education, Dennis working at Birmingham University in the department of computer science. I developed a late-start career in personnel management in the National Health Service, moving by degrees into training and ultimately into self-employment in organisation and personal development. Geoff after college set up a successful business until his untimely death in 1994. Drawing on Mark's experience, I encouraged Paul and Caroline to go through the psychological testing process that would help them find careers to suit their abilities – and so they have, and I am very proud of them. Paul is an agronomist managing projects overseas wherever sugar cane is grown – which seems to be on almost every continent now. He and Marilyn and their two children, our grandchildren James and Ellen, inevitably have a much travelled life, from a base in Oxfordshire. Caroline is a senior speech and language therapist in the NHS, a job she finds worthwhile even though it is a much less stable organisation than it used to be. She, Patrick and their two daughters Olivia and Rachel live a full life in Sheffield.

A part of me remained in Africa, though, and in 1985, as my son went to university, I started to wonder what had happened to Victoria and her similarly aged son and daughter, for whom she had had such educational ambitions. The letter I sent, to the last address I had, was the start of a correspondence that continued until her premature death from heart disease in 1989. It was the start, too, of many years of educational sponsorship with her family, first for her daughter Pearl at the only 'black' university then open to her, then nurse training for granddaughter Mandy, followed by college for Mandy's younger sister Beverly (Victoria loved to give all the children English as well as Xhosa names, and Mandy, I am proud to say, is called after me), and most recently school and university for Victoria's youngest granddaughter Siphokazi, born after her grandmother's death. We have given her the English name of Ursula, after my mother. Watching them grow and develop and make their way in the world, forging close family relationships with them as our visits have become more frequent, has been immensely satisfying.

Our first visit to South Africa, in 1997, after democracy had miraculously replaced apartheid, was an emotional one. There was the joy of meeting up with old friends, including Jiff and Alan Bowmaker, of seeing Dennis's son Dave and his family, of enjoying Cape Town's beauty once more. But my most vivid memory of that first trip is of stepping out of a little plane in East London in the Eastern Cape, to be met by Victoria's family. For those readers who did not live in South Africa under apartheid, it is impossible to describe the emotional impact of being able to walk into a restaurant with your new black friends to enjoy a meal, of being able to go with them to the best beach, of hearing their plans for a future unfettered by the old oppressions. In Cape Town we met up too with Vivian and her family, in particular her daughter Amanda, who now lives a successful life in Johannesburg with her husband Ike and three children.

I have lived in Britain for nearly 40 years now, and Dennis and I have returned to South Africa many times, always deriving great joy and satisfaction from old relationships sustained and new ones cemented. However, it feels too daunting, the idea of trying to revisit those harder-to-reach corners of Southern Africa where, as a young woman, I spent such vividly remembered years. The closest I have come to them has been through the world wide web. Besides, I find now that the act of writing this memoir was the journey I needed to make, so perhaps after all I have travelled enough.

EPILOGUE

Time Travelling with Google Earth

Fly to: < Mbala >

Select: < Mbala Zambia >
                   < Mbala Central African Republic >
                   < Mbala Chad >
                   < Mbala Cote d'Ivoire >
                   < Mbala Niger >

Click on   < Mbala Zambia >

The earth tilts, I'm flying
over France, a flash of Mediterranean
and look – the red brown of Africa, a scarf
of cloud over its tropical heart,
now diving down, down, a pixilated glimpse
of vast lake, before I'm led south-east,
am homing in on a tree-dotted grid
of rust-red tracks on sand.

Angular shadows of buildings like toy bricks,
the square of an office block, sprawling bungalows
that hug the shade of spreading trees.
Only my cursor moves. I point it north
and yes, here's the blue of little Chila,
scroll in closer to ruffled water, shallows fringed
with weed, and isn't that the shadow
of a slipway? and this a boathouse?

Pull out and draw the cursor back to town,
then east to zigzag on red roads, hovering
house by house until – it's this one, surely?
that familiar H-shape, the side garage,
a drive still circling a front patch of brown.
I scroll in, peering as the picture blurs, catch
myself searching for rose beds round a lawn,
a gardener with a hose, a small boy's trike,
a pram in the shade of the miombo trees.

ACKNOWLEDGEMENTS

During the journey of writing this memoir, my reading has filled some of the yawning gaps in my ignorance. The following have been especially valuable:

A History of Rhodesia Robert Blake, Eyre Methuen 1977: the full and authoritative history up to 1977.

The Past is Another Country Martin Meredith, Andre Deutsch 1979: Includes a detailed account of Southern Rhodesia in the run up to and during UDI.

The State of Africa: a history of 50 years of independence Martin Meredith, The Free Press 2005: Spans the whole continent over the second half of the 20th century.

Going Home Doris Lessing, Michael Joseph 1957: Lessing's clear-sighted descriptions of the people and country of 1950's Southern Rhodesia are full of insights.

The Africa House Christina Lamb, Viking 1999: True story of an English gentleman realising his dream of a grand estate in the African bush – not far from Abercorn.

House of Stone Christina Lamb, Harper Press 2007: Traces the intertwined lives of a white farmer and his family and their black nanny, examining how Rhodesia/Zimbabwe's long history of conflict comes to divide them.

Mukiwa – a white boy in Africa Peter Godwin, Picador 1996: memoir of growing up in Rhodesia, living and fighting through the country's vicious civil war.

Mimi and Toutou Go Forth – the bizarre battle for Lake Tanganyika Giles Foden, Penguin Books 2004: Hilarious, barely believable history of how a small group of eccentric Britons broke Germany's domination of the lake during World War I. S.S. Liemba in her previous incarnation stars.

Harvest of Thorns Shimmer Chinodya, Baobab Books 1989: A novel in a clear black Zimbabwean voice, covering the country's transition from civil war to independence and beyond.

Beloved African Jill Baker, Covos-Day Books 2000: Biography of John Hammond, committed to black education in a Southern Rhodesia increasingly beset by conflict between black and white, and between traditional and modern cultures.

The Dust Diaries Owen Sheers, Faber and Faber 2004: Part biography, part memoir, part travel book, based on the life of Arthur Shearly Cripps, poet and maverick missionary, vividly conjuring rural Mashonaland in the early 20th century.

Footprints in the Dust Ian Mackinson, Ian Mackinson 2003, Mutende, Mill Close, Nursling SO16 0XE: memoir of a long-serving administrator in the protectorate of Northern Rhodesia, full of vivid descriptions of life and service.

Blood River: a journey to Africa's broken heart Tim Butcher, Chatto and Windus 2007: gripping account of a journey tracing the river Congo from its source near Lake Tanganyika to the Atlantic ocean.

I have had help from many people as I mined my memories, wrote and rewrote this memoir. I am grateful to my brother Simon Watson and to Isabel Gillard, who read and commented on work in progress, Simon more than once; to John Watson for sharing his Rhodesian memories, anecdotes and photographs, and for his description of the roads; to Jiff and Alan Bowmaker, Colin Carlin and Ian and Barbara Mackinson for filling many a gap in my memories of Abercorn and its people. A special thanks to Jacky Medway, best possible writing partner, whose insights and gift for posing just the right question at the right moment played a vital part in my getting the project off the ground, and later breaking through 'stuck' moments.

Jayne Watson (no relation!) captured images for the chapter headings with both talent and patience at my numerous comments and requests for editing.